W9-CEY-157

Contents

Contents

Introduction

Even in the age of the supermarket, food lovers enjoy the changes the seasons bring to their tables, and most of our major food cultures are grounded in farming communities and peasant cookery. There is also, however, another kind of food seasonality – different styles of cooking come in and go out of favor according to the fashions of the time.

It's been fascinating in recent years to see the return of many of the old ways of cooking. Fast food seems to have been put in its place and 'slow' food to have joined it in the public consciousness as something both good for you and presentable at the table. Alongside quick pastas, speedy salads and wok-tossed minute meals now sit the slow and hearty fireside foods of old.

In the late 1960s and early '70s, the slow-cooking pot that once bubbled away for hours on the edge of the fireplace underwent an electronic conversion into the 'crockpot', and became very fashionable. People embraced an appliance that could slow-cook a wet meal automatically (usually without the need for stirring or watching over), allowing them to produce wonderful traditional family meals without being tied to the kitchen for the entire day. Like many innovations, however, the crockpot has become identified with the time of its invention and is now seen as old technology. Your mother probably still has one stashed in the back of her cupboard somewhere or gathering dust in the back shed – likely beige or burnt orange in color with a motif on the side.

Introduction

Well, slow cookers have had a makeover. Soups, casseroles, hearty stews and exotic tagines – the traditional 'slow' foods of all nations – are back on the food agenda and slow-cooked, inexpensive cuts of meat appear on the menus of some of the finest eateries around the Western world. So slow cookers are perfectly placed to again bubble happily away on the kitchen bench, imparting beautiful aromas to your kitchen while cooking unaided and unsupervised.

In short, the slow cooker is back, looking good and ready for service in the modern kitchen.

Once you've started using a slow cooker, you'll soon become a convert to its convenience and economy. It's a low-fuss appliance and a low-energy user – once the cooker reaches its set temperature, the food helps to retain its own heat and very little extra power is needed. Flavors are trapped inside the pot, and each ingredient imparts its character and takes on the flavors around it. Use good-quality stocks, fresh vegetables, citrus rinds and robust herbs such as rosemary and thyme for beautiful, old-fashioned dishes.

Another of the great attributes of the slow cooker is that it can provide the ultimate one-pot cooking technique, with only your cutting board, knife and plates to wash along with the cooker after dinner. There are few simpler and more fundamental ways of cooking.

Getting to Know Your Slow Cooker

There are only two heat settings on most slow cookers – 'low' and 'high'. Food will be brought to simmer on both settings; they merely determine the time taken to reach that simmer. It's advisable to preheat your slow cooker for 10 to 15 minutes before use to help food reach cooking temperature faster.

The various makes of slow cookers each respond a little differently – if your cooker is particularly large or low-powered, then you may need to add a little more cooking time than a recipe indicates. So, for the first few recipes, mark down your starting and finishing time in order to get a feel for how your particular cooker responds.

Keep an eye on the pot in the late stages of cooking, in case it requires more or less cooking time or a top-up of liquid. However, remember that your slow cooker cannot recover heat losses quickly, so lift the lid only when necessary. When you have to stir a dish, do it during the last few hours of cooking time or only when instructed in the recipe. If you need to remove the lid several times, you'll have to extend the cooking time a little. Soon you'll be able to tell if a meal needs extra time by simply looking at it in the late stages of cooking.

If your cooker has a removable ceramic bowl, it may be used in the oven – ideal when adding a pastry or cheese crust to your favorite stews. Just be careful not to place the ceramic insert on the stovetop or burners, as it will not withstand sudden temperature changes.

Getting to Know Your Slow Cooker

Your slow cooker is wonderful for cooking ahead for the freezer, or you can prepare double the usual quantity of a favorite casserole and freeze the extra amount. To freeze a slow-cooked dish that you plan to reheat in the slow cooker, turn the food out into a bowl, then allow the cooker's ceramic insert to cool before washing it, coating it with a little oil or butter and returning the food. Cover the insert and place in the freezer until the food is set, then transfer the frozen block of food to a large freezer bag. This way, when you return the food to the slow cooker for reheating it will always fit back in perfectly. Don't use the ceramic bowl for storing food in the freezer indefinitely.

To reheat a frozen meal, place in the slow cooker's ceramic container and place it in the oven. But always remember not to put frozen foods into a preheated cooker.

Adding Liquid

Your slow cooker should never be filled higher than 2 cm (¾ in) from the top – if it's too full the lid will lift while the food is cooking. If you need to top up the liquids during cooking, don't simply add cold water; boil the kettle. If you're using stock, heat it in a small saucepan before adding it.

Of course, you may sometimes end up with a recipe with too much liquid, since the liquid content of meats and vegetables varies. The excess can be reduced by removing the cover and setting the cooker on high for about 45 minutes. Keep in mind that most recipes cooked in the slow cooker will be juicier than if they were cooked conventionally, since the slow cooking prevents evaporation. For this reason, you can even cook without liquid. Fish and sausages, for example, can be placed in the cooker and cooked for 2 to 4 hours, depending on the thickness of the meat. New potatoes can be slow-cooked for 8 to 10 hours.

Roasts

The more fat or marbling the meat has, the less liquid you will need, as the natural fats help to baste and moisten the food. Roasts can thus be cooked on low without adding water, if desired. A small amount of water is recommended, though, as slow-cooked gravies are especially tasty – it would be a shame to leave them behind!

Gravy can be made right inside your cooker in three steps:

1 Remove the foods from the pot, leaving the juices.

2 Prepare a smooth paste of about 1/4 cup (2 oz) plain (all-purpose) flour or cornflour (cornstarch) to 1/4 cup (2 oz) water. Pour the mixture into the liquid in your cooker and stir well.

3 Turn the setting to high and cook, stirring occasionally, until mixture thickens and becomes slightly transparent (approximately 15 to 20 minutes). Then serve.

Meats generally slow-cook faster than most root vegetables, so it's a good idea to arrange the vegetables around the outer edges of the insert where the heating element is. Most vegetables should be cut into small pieces or at least quartered. Carrots and other dense root vegetables should be peeled and put where they'll be covered by liquid.

Adapting Your Favorite Recipes for the Slow Cooker

Due to their unique wraparound heating system and long cooking time, slow cooker temperatures cannot be equated to those of an oven or a frying pan. We've provided a cooking time conversion table on page 11, instead, so that you can prepare your favorite recipes in your slow cooker.

Small portions of food can be cooked in a slow cooker, but the times will vary. Because there is no direct heat at the bottom, the cooker must be at least half-full to meet the recommended times. It's better to adjust your recipe volume according to the size of your slow cooker.

There are two other basic rules that will help when you come to adapt recipes:

- Allow sufficient cooking time on a low setting, using the conversion table below.

- Reduce the amount of liquid prescribed by conventional recipes. Remember: liquids do not boil away in a slow cooker, so usually you'll have more liquid at the end of the cooking process rather than less. Generally, 1 to 2 cups (½–1 pint) of liquid are enough for any recipe, unless:

  - it contains rice, pasta or other absorbent grains (polenta, couscous, quinoa, etc.)

  - you're cooking a pot roast-style dish where you want to have liquids at the end in order to make gravy or sauce

  - it's a classic Italian-style 'bolito misto' dish where you simmer the meats and discard the liquid at the end of the cooking process.

Cooking Time Conversion Guide*

Oven or stovetop cooking time	Slow cooker low cooking time	Slow cooker high cooking time
15–30 mins	4–6 hrs	1½–2½ hrs
35–45 mins	6–8 hrs	3–4 hrs
50 mins–3 hrs	8–12 hrs	4–6 hrs

* This guide applies to casserole-type dishes. Most roasts will require at least 7 hours on low.

Cooking Time Conversion Guide

In the case of a pot roast, you can cook thirsty grains such as those mentioned above after removing the main joint of meat to be rested and carved. Simply turn the cooker to high, add the grains and cook for 45 minutes with the lid removed, and you have a thick, wet, rustic-style base for a truly old-fashioned meal.

If cooked rice is called for in the recipe you're adapting, you can stir raw rice in with other ingredients and add 1 cup (8 oz) of extra liquid per cup of raw rice. Use long-grain rice for best results in all-day cooking. If a recipe calls for dried beans, the beans should be soaked overnight, then cooked on high for 2 to 3 hours. Or you can cook the beans overnight on low or parboil them with water and 1 teaspoon of bicarbonate of soda (baking soda) added to speed up the breakdown of the beans.

As we mentioned earlier, slow cooking is often one-step cooking, so many steps in conventional recipes can be deleted – often you can put all the ingredients in the slow cooker at once then cook them for approximately 8 hours. There are a few important exceptions, however. Seafood or frozen vegetables cook quickly, so it is best to add them during the last hour of cooking. Do not precook them, just rinse and drain thoroughly before adding. And milk, sour cream and fresh cream should be added during the last half-hour of cooking.

Cooking Time Conversion Guide

It's preferable to use whole herbs and spices in the slow cooker.

For dumplings, drop spoonfuls of dumpling mixture into a simmering stew or liquid and cook, covered, for about 30 minutes on high.

When a dish is finished with a crisp topping of crumbs or grated cheese, you can transfer the slow cooker's bowl straight to the oven for browning if the bowl is removable, as mentioned earlier. If it isn't, you'll need to transfer the dish to a heatproof bowl first.

And one last word: some foods may not benefit from slow cooking, including:

• noodles

• macaroni

• crisp green vegetables

• Asian vegetables

• puddings or sauces made with a foundation of milk or cream.

Care must be taken when using these foods in slow cooker recipes.

Get Inventive!

With the guidelines in this introduction, you should be able to take any appropriate recipe and convert it for the slow cooker.

Think outside the square and make the slow cooker work for you. Try cooking porridge with dried fruit overnight for a hearty winter breakfast, or making a sweet snack to cook away as you settle into the sofa after the main meal – the applications are virtually unlimited.

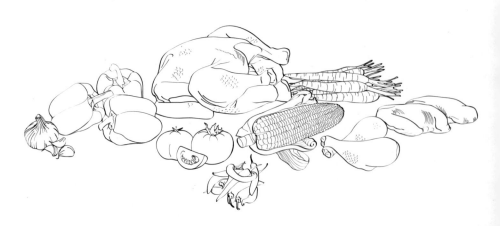

Types of Cookers

The slow cookers on the market vary in shape, size and capacity. When choosing one there are many points to consider. All cookers consume approximately the same amount of power, but the settings may vary.

As mentioned before, some cookers have a removable ceramic cooking bowl, which enables food to be easily browned or crisped under the grill (broiler) for final presentation. In these cookers, the heating elements are fitted within the walls of the base unit.

Another style of cooker has a ceramic bowl permanently fixed into the outer casing, with the heating elements placed between the outer casing and the cooking bowl. Some of these styles come with detachable power cords so that the unit can be easily taken to the table for serving.

Cooker capacity can vary from 1.5 to 6 quarts. While the little cookers may seem nifty and compact, it's usually best to get the largest size you think you can use. Once you become familiar with your cooker, you'll appreciate being able to cook double quantities and large joints of meat! It's an easy way to feed guests.

How to Clean and Care for Your Slow Cooker

Do not put frozen or very cold foods into a slow cooker if the unit has been preheated or is hot to the touch, and never submerge the cooking unit in water. If the ceramic bowl is removable, place it in the dishwasher; if not, wash it with hot soapy water as soon as possible after emptying it. Care should be taken to avoid chipping or cracking the cooker with metal spoons or water taps (faucets).

Do not pour cold water into a ceramic-lined cooker if it is hot, and do not use abrasive cleaning compounds. A cloth, sponge or rubber spatula will usually remove any food residue easily. If necessary, a plastic cleaning pad may be used. To remove water spots and other stains, use a non-abrasive cleaner or vinegar.

A metal-lined cooker may be cleaned with a damp cloth or scouring pad or sprayed lightly with an all-purpose cleaner.

Safety

When using electrical kitchen appliances, basic safety precautions should always be followed:

• Read all instructions.

• Use your slow cooker on an even and stable surface.

• Do not place the slow cooker on or near a hot gas or electric burner or into a heated oven. (Only heatproof ceramic inserts can be placed in the oven or under a grill (broiler).)

• Do not touch hot surfaces – always use handles or knobs.

• Use caution when moving the slow cooker if it contains hot oil or hot liquids.

• Ensure close supervision when the slow cooker is used by or near children.

• Unplug the slow cooker from the power outlet when not in use, before cleaning, and before putting on or taking off parts.

Appetizers, Snacks & Dips

Beefy Cheese Dip

- 1 pound lean ground beef   455 g
- 1 small onion, very finely chopped
- 2 (16 ounce) package cubed Velveeta® cheese   2 (455 g)
- 2 (10 ounce) cans diced tomatoes and green chilies   2 (280 g)
- 1 teaspoon minced garlic   5 ml
- Tortilla chips

Cook beef in skillet on low heat for 10 minutes and break up large meat chunks. Transfer to sprayed 4-quart (4 L) slow cooker.

Add onion, cheese, tomatoes and green chilies, and garlic. Stir well, cover and cook on LOW for 1 hour. Serve with tortilla chips. Serves 6 to 8.

Hot Broccoli Dip

- 1 (16 ounce) box Mexican Velveeta® cheese, cubed   455 g
- 1 (10 ounce) can golden mushroom soup   280 g
- ¼ cup milk   60 ml
- 1 (10 ounce) box frozen chopped broccoli, thawed   280 g

Combine cheese, soup and milk in sprayed slow cooker, stir well and fold in broccoli. Cover and cook on LOW for 1 to 2 hours. Stir before serving. Serves 8 to 10.

18

Broccoli-Veggie Dip

- ¾ cup (1½ sticks) butter   170 g
- 3 ribs celery, chopped
- 6 button mushrooms, stemmed, chopped
- 1 bunch green onions with tops, finely chopped
- 3 tablespoons flour   20 g
- 1 (10 ounce) can cream of chicken soup   280 g
- 1 (10 ounce) box chopped broccoli, thawed   280 g
- 1 (5 ounce) garlic cheese roll, cut in chunks   145 g
- Wheat crackers or corn chips

Melt butter in skillet and saute celery, mushrooms and onion, but do not brown; stir in flour. Spoon into sprayed, small slow cooker, stir in remaining ingredients and mix well.

Cover and cook on LOW for 2 to 3 hours and stir several times. Serve with wheat crackers or corn chips. Serves 6 to 8.

All slow cooker recipes for appetizers, snacks and dips work well in a 2 to 3.5 quart (2 to 3.5 L) slow cooker.

Chili-Cheese Dipper

- **2 (15 ounce) cans chili**   2 (425 g)
- **1 (10 ounce) can tomatoes and green chilies**   280 g
- **1 (16 ounce) package cubed Velveeta® cheese**   455 g
- **1 onion, chopped**

Place all ingredients in sprayed slow cooker. Cover and cook on LOW for
1 hour to 1 hour 30 minutes. Serve right from slow cooker. Stir before serving.
Serves 6 to 8.

Indian-Corn Dip

- **1 pound lean ground beef**   455 g
- **1 onion, finely chopped**
- **1 (15 ounce) can whole kernel corn, drained**   425 g
- **1 (16 ounce) jar salsa**   455 g
- **1 (1 pound) package cubed Velveeta® cheese**   455 g
- **Tortilla chips**

Brown and cook beef in skillet on low heat for about 10 minutes and drain.
Transfer to sprayed slow cooker and add onion, corn, salsa and cheese.

Cover and cook on LOW for 1 hour, remove lid and stir. Serve with tortilla chips.
Serves 6 to 8.

Cheesy Bacon Dip

- **2 (8 ounce) packages cream cheese, softened**   **2 (225 g)**
- **1 (8 ounce) package shredded colby Jack cheese**   **225 g**
- **2 tablespoons mustard**   **30 ml**
- **2 teaspoons marinade for chicken**   **10 ml**
- **4 fresh green onions with tops, sliced**
- **1 pound bacon, cooked, crumbled**   **455 g**
- **Rye or pumpernickel bread**

Cut cream cheese into cubes and place in 4 to 5-quart (4 to 5 L) slow cooker. Add colby Jack cheese, mustard, marinade for chicken, green onions and ¼ teaspoon (1 ml) salt.

Cover and cook on LOW for 1 hour and stir to melt cheese. Stir in crumbled bacon. Serve with small-size rye bread or toasted pumpernickel bread. Serves 6 to 8.

Mexican Bacon-Cheese Dip

- **1 (16 ounce) package cubed Mexican Velveeta® cheese**   **455 g**
- **1 (10 ounce) can tomatoes and green chilies**   **280 g**
- **2 teaspoons Worcestershire sauce**   **10 ml**
- **1 pickled jalapeno, seeded, veined, chopped**
- **½ teaspoon dried mustard**   **2 ml**
- **½ cup whipping cream or half-and-half cream**   **40 g**
- **16 slices bacon, cooked, crumbled, divided**

Combine cubed cheese, tomatoes and green chilies, jalapeno, Worcestershire, mustard and half-and-half cream to sprayed, small slow cooker.

Turn heat to LOW, cover and cook for about 1 hour, stirring several times to make sure cheese melts.

While cheese is melting, place bacon in skillet, fry, drain and crumble.

Fold three-fourths of bacon into cheese mixture. When ready to "dip", sprinkle remaining bacon on top and serve from slow cooker. Serves 4 to 6.

Chicken-Enchilada Dip

- **2 pounds boneless, skinless chicken thighs, cubed**   **910 g**
- **1 (10 ounce) can enchilada sauce**   **280 g**
- **1 (7 ounce) can chopped green chilies, drained**   **195 g**
- **1 small onion, finely chopped**
- **1 large red bell pepper, seeded, finely chopped**
- **2 (8 ounce) packages cream cheese, cubed**   **2 (225 g)**
- **1 (16 ounce) package shredded American cheese**   **455 g**
- **Tortilla chips**

Place chicken thighs, enchilada sauce, green chilies, onion and bell pepper in sprayed 4 to 5-quart (4 to 5 L) slow cooker.

Cover and cook on LOW for 4 to 6 hours. Stir in cream cheese and American cheese and cook for additional 30 minutes. Stir several times during cooking. Serve with tortilla chips. Serves 8 to 10.

Creamy Pepperoni Dip

- 1 (6 ounce) package pepperoni   170 g
- 1 bunch fresh green onions, thinly sliced
- 1 green bell pepper, seeded, cored, finely chopped
- 1 medium tomato, finely chopped
- 1 (14 ounce) jar pizza sauce   395 g
- 1½ cups shredded mozzarella cheese   170 g
- 1 (8 ounce) package cream cheese, cubed   225 g
- Wheat crackers or tortilla chips

Chop pepperoni into small pieces and place in sprayed, small slow cooker. Add onion, bell pepper, tomato and pizza sauce and stir well.

Cover and cook on LOW for 2 hours 30 minutes to 3 hours 30 minutes.

Stir in mozzarella and cream cheese and stir until they melt. Serve with wheat crackers or tortilla chips. Serves 4 to 6.

Sausage-Hamburger Dip

- 1 pound bulk pork sausage   455 g
- 1 pound lean ground beef   455 g
- 1 cup hot salsa   265 g
- 1 (10 ounce) can cream of mushroom soup   280 g
- 1 (10 ounce) can tomatoes and green chilies   280 g
- 1 teaspoon garlic powder   5 ml
- ¾ teaspoon ground oregano   4 ml
- 2 (16 ounce) packages cubed Velveeta® cheese   2 (455 g)

Cook sausage and ground beef in large skillet for 15 minutes and drain. Place in sprayed 4 to 5-quart (4 to 5 L) slow cooker.

Add salsa, mushroom soup, tomatoes and green chilies, garlic powder and oregano; stir well. Fold in cheese.

Cover and cook on LOW for 1 hour or until cheese melts. Stir once during cooking time. Serve from cooker. Serves 8 to 10.

Sausage-Cheese Dip

- **1 pound hot sausage**   **455 g**
- **1 (10 ounce) can chopped tomatoes and green chilies**   **280 g**
- **1 (2 pound) box Velveeta® cheese**   **910 g**

Brown and cook sausage in skillet, drain and place in sprayed, small slow cooker. Stir in tomatoes and green chilies and mix well.

Cut cheese into chunks and add to sausage-tomato mixture. Cover and cook on LOW for 1 hour or until cheese melts.

Stir when ready to serve and serve hot in slow cooker. Serves 4 to 6.

Party Smokies

- **1 cup ketchup**   **270 g**
- **1 cup plum jelly**   **320 g**
- **1 tablespoon lemon juice**   **15 ml**
- **2 (5 ounce) packages tiny smoked sausages**   **2 (145 g)**

Combine all ingredients in sprayed, small slow cooker. Cover and cook on LOW for 1 hour. Stir before serving. Serve right from cooker. Serves 4 to 6.

Sausage-Pineapple Bits

The "sweet and hot" makes a delicious combo.

• **1 (1 pound) link cooked Polish sausage, skinned**	**455 g**
• **1 (1 pound) hot bulk sausage**	**455 g**
• **1 (8 ounce) can crushed pineapple with juice**	**225 g**
• **1 cup apricot preserves**	**320 g**
• **1 tablespoon marinade for chicken**	**15 ml**
• **1½ cups packed brown sugar**	**330 g**

Slice link sausage into ½-inch (1.2 cm) pieces. Shape bulk sausage into 1-inch (2.5 cm) balls and brown in skillet.

Combine sausage pieces, sausage balls, pineapple, apricot preserves, marinade for chicken and brown sugar in sprayed slow cooker. Stir gently so meatballs do not break up.

Cover and cook on LOW for 1 hour 30 minutes to 2 hours. Serves 8 to 10.

All slow cooker recipes for appetizers, snacks and dips work well in a 2 to 3.5 quart (2 to 3.5 L) slow cooker.

Easy Hot Dog Fondue

- 1 (14 ounce) jar Cheez Whiz®   395 g
- 2 tablespoons milk   30 ml
- 1 teaspoon chili powder   5 ml
- 1 teaspoon cayenne pepper   5 ml
- 1 (16 ounce) package beef franks   455 g
- 1 (10 ounce) package pretzel sticks   280 g

Place Cheez Whiz®, milk, chili powder and cayenne pepper in small, sprayed slow cooker. Cover and cook on LOW for 1 to 2 hours or until hot and steamy.

Cook franks according to package directions and drain. Cut each frank into about 4 pieces and place pretzel stick in each for dipping. Serves 6 to 8.

Spicy Franks

- 1 cup packed brown sugar   220 g
- 1 cup chili sauce   270 g
- 1 tablespoon red wine vinegar   15 ml
- 2 teaspoons teriyaki sauce   10 ml
- 2 teaspoons dijon-style mustard   10 ml
- 2 (12 ounce) packages frankfurters   2 (340 g)

Combine brown sugar, chili sauce, vinegar, soy sauce and mustard in small, sprayed slow cooker and mix well. Cut frankfurters diagonally in 1-inch (2.5 cm) pieces. Stir in frankfurters.

Cover and cook on LOW for 1 to 2 hours. Serve from cooker using cocktail picks. Serves 4.

The word "Crock-Pot®" is a trademark of Rival Manufacturing Company and refers to the crockery insert of its appliance with heating elements in the sides and bottom.

Bubbly Bourbon Franks

- 1 (1 pound) package wieners   455 g
- 1 onion, chopped
- ½ cup chili sauce   135 g
- ⅔ cup packed brown sugar   150 g
- ½ cup bourbon   125 ml

Cut wieners diagonally into bite-size pieces. Combine onion, chili sauce, brown sugar and bourbon in sprayed, small slow cooker.

Stir in wieners. Cover and cook on LOW for 1 to 2 hours. Serve in chafing dish. Serves 6 to 8.

Hot Reuben Spread

- 1 (8 ounce) package shredded Swiss cheese   225 g
- ¾ cup drained sauerkraut, rinsed, drained   110 g
- 1 (8 ounce) package cream cheese, softened, cubed   225 g
- 2 (2.5 ounce) packages sliced corned beef, chopped   2 (70 g)
- Rye bread

Combine Swiss cheese, sauerkraut, cream cheese and corned beef in bowl and spoon into sprayed, small slow cooker.

Cover and cook on LOW for 1 hour. Serve on slices of 3-inch (8 cm) rye bread. Serves 4 to 6.

Teriyaki Wings

- **2½ pounds chicken wingettes**   **1.2 kg**
- **1 onion, chopped**
- **1 cup soy sauce**   **250 ml**
- **1 cup packed brown sugar**   **220 g**
- **1 teaspoon minced garlic**   **5 ml**
- **1½ teaspoons ground ginger**   **7 ml**

Rinse chicken and pat dry. Place chicken wingettes on broiler pan and broil for about 10 minutes on both sides.

Transfer wingettes to sprayed, large slow cooker. Combine onion, soy sauce, brown sugar, garlic and ginger in bowl. Spoon sauce over wingettes.

Cover and cook on HIGH for 2 hours. Stir wingettes once during cooking to coat chicken evenly with sauce. Serves 8 to 10.

Wings in Honey Sauce

- **1 (2 pound) package chicken wingettes**   910 g
- **2 cups honey**   680 g
- **¾ cup soy sauce**   175 ml
- **¾ cup chili sauce**   205 g
- **¼ cup canola oil**   60 ml
- **1 teaspoon minced garlic**   5 ml
- **Dried parsley flakes**

Rinse chicken, pat dry and sprinkle with a little salt and pepper. Place wingettes in broiler pan and broil for 20 minutes (10 minutes on each side) or until light brown.

Transfer to sprayed slow cooker. Combine honey, soy sauce, chili sauce, oil and garlic in bowl and spoon over wingettes.

Cover and cook on LOW for 4 to 5 hours or on HIGH for 2 hours to 2 hours 30 minutes. Garnish with dried parsley flakes, if desired. Serves 8 to 10.

> *All slow cooker recipes for appetizers, snacks and dips work well in a 2 to 3.5 quart (2 to 3.5 L) slow cooker.*

Buffalo Hot Wings

- **3 pounds chicken wings**   **1.4 kg**
- **2 cups barbecue sauce**   **530 g**
- **¼ - ½ cup Frank's® Hot Wings Sauce**   **60 - 125 ml**
- **2 tablespoons light brown sugar**   **30 g**
- **1 tablespoon prepared mustard**   **15 ml**

Preheat oven to broil. Remove wing tips and place wings in roasting pan. Place in oven under broiler about 5 inches and brown on both sides (about 5 minutes per side).

Mix barbecue sauce, hot wings sauce, light brown sugar and mustard in bowl. Drain wings and place in sprayed slow cooker. Pour sauce mixture over top.

Cover and cook on LOW about 5 to 6 hours or until juices of chicken run clear. Before serving, separate wings at joints. (It's easier to separate after they cook.) Serves about 8 to 10.

Crab-Artichoke Spread

- 1 (6 ounce) can crabmeat, flaked 170 g
- ½ cup grated parmesan cheese 50 g
- 1 bunch fresh green onions, sliced
- 1½ tablespoons lemon juice 22 ml
- 1 (15 ounce) can artichoke hearts, drained, finely chopped 425 g
- 1 (8 ounce) package cream cheese, cubed 225 g
- Toasted bagel chips

Combine all ingredients in sprayed, small slow cooker and stir well.

Cover and cook on LOW for 1 hour to 1 hour 30 minutes. Stir until cream cheese mixes well. Serve on toasted bagel chips. Serves 4 to 6.

Unbelievable Crab Dip

- 1 (6 ounce) can white crabmeat, drained, flaked 2 (170 g)
- 1 (8 ounce) package cream cheese, softened 225 g
- ½ cup (1 stick) butter, sliced 115 g
- 2 tablespoons white cooking wine 30 ml
- Chips or crackers

Combine crabmeat, cream cheese, butter and wine in sprayed, small slow cooker.

Cover and cook on LOW for 1 hour and gently stir to combine all ingredients. Serve from cooker with chips or crackers. Serves 4 to 6.

Because slow cookers cook differently, check to see if item is done at the shortest cooking time.

Creamy Crab Dip

- **1 (8 ounce) and 1 (3 ounce) packages cream cheese, softened**   **225 g/85 g**
- **⅔ cup mayonnaise**   **150 g**
- **1 tablespoon marinade for chicken**   **15 ml**
- **3 fresh green onions with tops, chopped**
- **2 (6 ounce) cans crabmeat, drained, flaked**   **2 (170 g)**

Combine cream cheese, mayonnaise, 1 teaspoon (5 ml) salt and marinade for chicken in bowl and mix well with fork.

Stir in sherry, onions and crabmeat and spoon into sprayed, small slow cooker.

Cover and cook on LOW for 1 hour 30 minutes to 2 hours and stir once.
Serves 6 to 8.

All slow cooker recipes for appetizers, snacks and dips work well in a 2 to 3.5 quart (2 to 3.5 L) slow cooker.

Soups,
Stews, Chilis
& Chowders

Cheddar-Chicken Soup

- 2 cups milk   **500 ml**
- 1 (7 ounce) package cheddar-broccoli soup starter   **200 g**
- 1 cup cooked, finely chopped chicken breasts   **140 g**
- 1 (10 ounce) frozen green peas, thawed   **280 g**
- Shredded cheddar cheese

Place 5 cups (1.2 L) water and milk in sprayed slow cooker. Set heat on HIGH until water and milk come to a boil.

Stir contents of soup starter into hot water and milk and stir well. Add chopped chicken, green peas and a little salt and pepper.

Cover and cook on LOW for 2 to 3 hours. To serve, sprinkle cheddar cheese over each serving of soup. Serves 4.

Meaty Cabbage Soup

- 1 pound lean ground beef   **455 g**
- 1 small head cabbage, chopped
- 2 (15 ounce) cans jalapeno pinto beans with liquid   **2 (425 g)**
- 1 (15 ounce) can tomato sauce   **425 g**
- 1 (15 ounce) can Mexican stewed tomatoes   **425 g**
- 1 (14 ounce) can beef broth   **395 g**
- 2 teaspoons ground cumin   **10 ml**

Brown ground beef in skillet, drain and place in sprayed 5 to 6-quart (5 to 6 L) slow cooker.

Add cabbage, beans, tomato sauce, tomatoes, broth, cumin and 1 cup (250 ml) water and mix well. Cover and cook on LOW for 5 to 6 hours or until cabbage is tender. Serves 4 to 6.

Every time the lid is lifted, heat is lost; keep the lid on or add 15 to 20 minutes to cooking time each time you peek.

A+ Broccoli-Cheese Soup

- 1 (16 ounce) package frozen chopped broccoli, thawed   455 g
- 1 (12 ounce) package cubed Velveeta® cheese   340 g
- 1 (2 ounce) packet white sauce mix   60 g
- 1 (1 ounce) packet vegetable soup mix   30 g
- 1 (12 ounce) can evaporated milk   375 ml
- 1 (14 ounce) can chicken broth   395 g

Combine all ingredients plus 2 cups (500 ml) water in sprayed, large slow cooker and stir well.

Cover and cook on LOW for 6 to 7 hours or on HIGH for 3 hours 30 minutes to 4 hours. Stir for 1 hour before serving time. Serves 4 to 6.

Pizza Soup

- 3 (10 ounce) cans tomato bisque soup   3 (280 g)
- 1 (10 ounce) can French onion soup   280 g
- 2 teaspoons Italian seasoning   10 ml
- ¾ cup tiny pasta shells   80 g
- 1½ cups shredded mozzarella cheese   170 g

Combine soups, Italian seasoning and 1½ soup cans water in sprayed 4 to 5-quart (4 to 5 L) slow cooker. Cover and cook on HIGH for 1 hour or until mixture is hot.

Add pasta shells and cook for 1 hour 30 minutes to 2 hours or until pasta is cooked.

Stir several times to keep pasta from sticking to bottom of slow cooker. Turn heat off, add mozzarella cheese and stir until cheese melts. Serves 6 to 8.

TIP: *For a special way to serve this soup, sprinkle some french-fried onions over top of each serving.*

It saves calories to use neufchatel cheese instead of cream cheese.

Pasta-Veggie Soup

- 2 yellow squash, peeled, chopped
- 2 zucchini, sliced
- 1 (10 ounce) package frozen whole kernel corn, thawed   280 g
- 1 red bell pepper, chopped
- 1 (15 ounce) can stewed tomatoes   425 g
- 1 teaspoon Italian seasoning   5 ml
- 2 teaspoons dried oregano   10 ml
- 2 (14 ounce) cans beef broth   2 (395 g)
- ¾ cup small shell pasta   80 g
- Shredded mozzarella cheese

Combine squash, zucchini, corn, bell pepper, tomatoes, Italian seasoning, oregano, broth and 2 cups (500 ml) water in sprayed 6-quart (6 L) slow cooker.

Cover and cook on LOW for 6 to 7 hours.

Add pasta shells and cook for additional 30 to 45 minutes or until pasta is tender. Garnish with a sprinkle of shredded mozzarella cheese on each bowl of soup. Serves 4 to 5.

Recipes in this cookbook may be cooked in 3 to 6-quart slow cookers. You may need to adjust the quantity of ingredients for a smaller cooker.

Spinach-Tortellini Soup

- 1 (1 ounce) packet white sauce mix   30 g
- 3 boneless, skinless chicken breast halves
- 1 (14 ounce) can chicken broth   395 g
- 1 teaspoon minced garlic   5 ml
- ½ teaspoon dried basil   2 ml
- ½ teaspoon cayenne pepper   2 ml
- 1 (8 ounce) package cheese tortellini   225 g
- 1½ cups half-and-half cream   375 ml
- 6 cups fresh baby spinach   180 g

Place white sauce mix in sprayed 5 to 6-quart (5 to 6 L) slow cooker. Stir in 4 cups (1 L) water and stir gradually until mixture is smooth.

Cut chicken into 1-inch (2.5 cm) pieces. Add chicken, broth, garlic, basil, oregano, cayenne pepper and ½ teaspoon (2 ml) salt to mixture.

Cover and cook on LOW for 6 to 7 hours or on HIGH for 3 hours. Stir in tortellini, cover and cook for additional 1 hour on HIGH.

Stir in cream and fresh spinach and cook just enough for soup to get hot. Serves 4 to 6.

TIP: A little shredded parmesan cheese on top of each serving is a nice touch.

Cooking time on HIGH equals about half the cooking time on LOW.

Cream of Zucchini Soup

- 1 small onion, very finely chopped
- 3½ - 4 cups grated zucchini with peels   440 - 500 g
- 2 (14 ounce) cans chicken broth   2 (395 g)
- 1 teaspoon seasoned salt   5 ml
- 1 teaspoon dried dill weed   5 ml
- ½ teaspoon white pepper   2 ml
- 2 tablespoons butter, melted   30 g
- 1 (8 ounce) carton sour cream   225 g

Combine all ingredients except sour cream in sprayed, small slow cooker. Cover and cook on LOW for 2 hours.

Fold in sour cream and continue cooking for about 10 minutes or just until soup is hot. Serves 4.

Minestrone Soup

- 2 (15 ounce) cans Italian stewed tomatoes   2 (425 g)
- 2 (16 ounce) packages frozen vegetables and
  pasta seasoned sauce   2 (455 g)
- 3 (14 ounce) cans beef broth   3 (395 g)
- 2 ribs celery, chopped
- 2 potatoes, peeled, cubed
- 1 teaspoon Italian herb seasoning   5 ml
- 2 (15 ounce) cans kidney beans, drained, rinsed   2 (425 g)
- 2 teaspoons minced garlic   10 ml

Combine tomatoes, vegetables, broth, celery, potatoes, seasoning, beans, garlic and 1 cup (250 ml) water in sprayed, large slow cooker and mix well.

Cover and cook on LOW for 4 to 6 hours. Serves 8 to 10.

If you don't want to use wine in a recipe, substitute water or chicken broth.

Hearty Vegetable-Spinach Soup

- 1 pound Italian sausage links   455 g
- 2 medium potatoes, peeled
- 2½ cups butternut or acorn squash   285 g
- 1 onion, chopped
- 1 (15 ounce) can kidney beans, rinsed, drained   425 g
- 2 teaspoons minced garlic   10 ml
- 1 teaspoon Italian seasoning   5 ml
- 2 (14 ounce) cans chicken broth   2 (395 g)
- 1 cup dry white wine   250 ml
- 3 - 4 cups fresh spinach   90 - 120 g

Cut sausage and potatoes into ½-inch (1.2 cm) slices. Cook sausage in skillet until brown and drain.

Combine squash, potatoes, onion, beans, garlic and Italian seasoning in sprayed, large slow cooker.

Top with sausage and pour chicken broth and wine over all. Cover and cook on LOW for 7 to 9 hours.

Stir in spinach, cover and cook for additional 10 minutes. Serves 6 to 8.

Vegetable-Lentil Soup

- 2 (19 ounce) cans lentil home-style soup   2 (540 g)
- 1 (15 ounce) can stewed tomatoes   425 g
- 1 (14 ounce) can chicken broth   395 g
- 1 onion, chopped
- 1 green bell pepper, chopped
- 3 ribs celery, sliced
- 1 carrot, halved lengthwise, sliced
- 2 teaspoons minced garlic   10 ml
- 1 teaspoon dried marjoram leaves   5 ml

Combine all ingredients in sprayed slow cooker and stir well.

Cover and cook on LOW for 5 to 6 hours. Serves 6 to 8.

Creamy Vegetable Soup

- 3 (14 ounce) cans chicken broth   3 (395 g)
- ¼ cup (½ stick) butter, melted   60 g
- 1 (16 ounce) package frozen mixed vegetables   455 g
- 1 onion, chopped
- 3 ribs celery, sliced
- 1 teaspoon ground cumin   5 ml
- 3 zucchini, coarsely chopped
- 2 cups chopped, fresh broccoli   180 g
- 1 cup half-and-half cream   250 ml

Combine broth, butter, vegetables, onion, celery, cumin, 1 teaspoon (5 ml) each of salt and pepper in sprayed, large slow cooker and stir well.

Cover and cook on LOW for 6 to 7 hours or on HIGH for 3 to 4 hours.

Stir in zucchini and broccoli. If not using HIGH temperature, turn heat to HIGH and cook for additional 30 minutes to 1 hour or until broccoli is tender-crisp.

Turn off heat and stir in half-and-half cream. Let stand for 10 minutes before serving. Serves 6 to 8.

Creamy Ham-Potato Soup

- 5 medium potatoes, peeled, cubed
- 2 cups cooked, cubed ham   280 g
- 1 cup fresh broccoli florets, cut very, very fine   70 g
- 1 (10 ounce) can cheddar cheese soup   280 g
- 1 (10 ounce) can fiesta nacho cheese soup   280 g
- 1 (14 ounce) can chicken broth   395 g
- 2½ soup cans milk
- Paprika

Place potatoes, ham and broccoli in sprayed slow cooker. Combine soups and milk in saucepan. Heat just enough to mix until smooth. Stir into ingredients already in slow cooker.

Cover and cook on LOW for 7 to 9 hours. When serving, sprinkle a little paprika over each serving. Serves 6 to 8.

Cheesy Potato Soup

- 6 medium potatoes, peeled, cubed
- 1 onion, very finely chopped
- 2 (14 ounce) cans chicken broth   2 (395 g)
- 1 (8 ounce) package shredded American cheese   225 g
- 1 cup half-and-half cream   250 ml

Combine potatoes, onion, chicken broth and pepper in sprayed slow cooker. Cover and cook on LOW for 8 to 10 hours. Mash potatoes in slow cooker.

About 1 hour before serving, stir in cheese and cream and cook for additional 1 hour. Serves 4 to 6.

It is best to check your seasonings after cooking. Sometimes over long periods of time the flavors may cook out and you may need to add some seasonings again.

Potato and Leek Soup

- **1 (1 ounce) packet white sauce mix**   **30 g**
- **1 (28 ounce) package frozen hash-brown potatoes with onions and peppers**   **795 g**
- **3 medium leeks, sliced**
- **3 cups cooked, cubed ham**   **420 g**
- **1 (12 ounce) can evaporated milk**   **375 ml**
- **1 (8 ounce) carton sour cream**   **225 g**

Pour 3 cups (750 ml) water in sprayed 4 to 5-quart (4 to 5 L) slow cooker and stir white sauce until smooth.

Add hash-brown potatoes, leeks, ham and evaporated milk. Cover and cook on LOW for 7 to 9 hours or on HIGH for 3 hours 30 minutes to 4 hours 30 minutes.

When ready to serve, turn heat to HIGH. Take out about 2 cups (500 ml) hot soup and pour into separate bowl. Stir in sour cream and return to cooker.

Cover and cook for additional 15 minutes or until mixture is thoroughly hot. Serves 6 to 8.

French Onion Soup

- 5 - 6 sweet onions, thinly sliced
- 1 clove garlic, minced
- 2 tablespoons butter   30 g
- 2 (14 ounce) cans beef broth   2 (395 g)
- 2 teaspoons Worcestershire sauce   10 ml
- 6 - 8 (1 inch) slices French bread   6 - 8 (2.5 cm)
- 8 slices Swiss cheese

Cook onions and garlic in large skillet on low heat (DO NOT BROWN) in hot butter for about 20 minutes and stir several times.

Transfer onion mixture to sprayed 4 to 5-quart (4 to 5 L) slow cooker. Add beef broth, Worcestershire and 1 cup (250 ml) water.

Cover and cook on LOW for 5 to 8 hours or on HIGH for 2 hours 30 minutes to 4 hours.

Before serving soup, toast bread slices with cheese slice on top. Broil for 3 to 4 minutes or until cheese is light brown and bubbly.

Ladle soup into bowls and top with toast. Serves 6 to 8.

Navy Bean Soup

- **8 slices thick-cut bacon, divided**
- **1 carrot**
- **3 (15 ounce) cans navy beans with liquid**   3 (425 g)
- **3 ribs celery, chopped**
- **1 onion, chopped**
- **2 (15 ounce) cans chicken broth**   2 (425 g)
- **1 teaspoon Italian herb seasoning**   5 ml
- **1 (10 ounce) can cream of chicken soup**   280 g

Cook bacon in skillet, drain and crumble. (Reserve 2 crumbled slices for garnish.) Cut carrot in half lengthwise and slice.

Combine most of crumbled bacon, carrot, beans, celery, onion, broth, seasoning, 1 cup (250 ml) water in sprayed 5 to 6-quart (5 to 6 L) slow cooker and stir to mix.

Cover and cook on LOW for 5 to 6 hours.

Ladle 2 cups (500 ml) soup mixture into food processor or blender and process until smooth.

Return to cooker, add cream of chicken soup and stir to mix. Turn heat to HIGH and cook for additional 10 to 15 minutes. Serves 6 to 8.

Italian Bean Soup

- 2 (15 ounce) cans great northern beans with liquid   2 (425 g)
- 2 (15 ounce) cans pinto beans with liquid   2 (425 g)
- 1 large onion, chopped
- 1 tablespoon instant beef bouillon granules   15 ml
- 1 tablespoon minced garlic   15 ml
- 2 teaspoons Italian seasoning   10 ml
- 2 (15 ounce) cans Italian stewed tomatoes   2 (425 g)
- 1 (15 ounce) can cut green beans, drained   425 g

Combine northern beans, pinto beans, onion, beef bouillon, garlic, Italian seasoning and 2 cups (500 ml) water in sprayed, large slow cooker.

Cover and cook on LOW for 6 to 8 hours.

Turn heat to HIGH, add stewed tomatoes and green beans and stir well. Continue cooking for additional 30 minutes or until green beans are tender. Serves 6 to 8.

TIP: Serve with crispy Italian toast.

Black Bean Soup with Sausage

- 1 pound hot sausage   455 g
- 1 onion, chopped
- 2 ribs celery, chopped
- 2 (14 ounce) cans chicken broth   2 (395 g)
- 2 (15 ounce) cans Mexican stewed tomatoes   2 (425 g)
- 1 green bell pepper, seeded, chopped
- 2 (15 ounce) cans black beans, rinsed, drained   2 (425 g)

Break up sausage and brown with onion and celery in large skillet. Drain off fat and place in sprayed, large slow cooker.

Add chicken broth, stewed tomatoes, bell pepper, black beans and 1 cup (250 ml) water. Cover and cook on LOW for 3 to 5 hours. Serves 4 to 6.

Black Bean Soup

- 2 (14 ounce) cans chicken broth   2 (395 g)
- 3 (15 ounce) cans black beans, rinsed, drained   3 (425 g)
- 2 (10 ounce) cans tomatoes and green chilies   2 (280 g)
- 1 onion, chopped
- 1 teaspoon ground cumin   5 ml
- ½ teaspoon dried thyme   2 ml
- ½ teaspoon dried oregano   2 ml
- 2 - 3 cups cooked, finely diced ham   280 - 420 g

Combine chicken broth and black beans in sprayed slow cooker and turn cooker to HIGH.

Cook just long enough for ingredients to get hot. Mash about half of beans in cooker.

Reduce heat to LOW and add tomatoes and green chilies, onion, cumin, thyme, oregano, ham and ¾ cup (175 ml) water.

Cover and cook for 5 to 6 hours. Serves 6 to 8.

Black-Eyed Soup

- 5 slices thick-cut bacon, diced
- 1 onion, chopped
- 1 green bell pepper, chopped
- 3 ribs celery, sliced
- 3 (15 ounce) cans jalapeno black-eyed peas with liquid   3 (425 g)
- 2 (15 ounce) cans stewed tomatoes with liquid   2 (425 g)
- 1 teaspoon chicken seasoning   5 ml

Cook bacon pieces in skillet until crisp, drain on paper towel and place in slow cooker. With bacon drippings in skillet, saute onion and bell peppers, but do not brown.

Add onions, bell pepper, celery, black-eyed peas, stewed tomatoes, 1½ cups (375 ml) water and chicken seasoning to sprayed slow cooker.

Cover and cook on LOW for 3 to 4 hours. Serves 6 to 8.

Cajun Bean Soup

- 1 (20 ounce) package Cajun-flavored 16-bean soup mix
  with flavor packet   570 g
- 2 cups cooked, finely chopped ham   280 g
- 1 chopped onion
- 2 (15 ounce) cans stewed tomatoes   2 (425 g)
- Cornbread

Soak beans overnight in sprayed, large slow cooker. After soaking, drain water and cover with 2 inches water over beans.

Cover and cook on LOW for 5 to 6 hours or until beans are tender. Add ham, onion, stewed tomatoes and flavor packet in bean soup mix.

Cover and cook on HIGH for 30 to 45 minutes. Serve with cornbread. Serves 4 to 6.

Barley-Bean Duo

- 2 (15 ounce) cans pinto beans with liquid   2 (425 g)
- 1 onion, chopped
- 2 ribs celery, chopped
- 3 (14 ounce) cans chicken broth   3 (395 g)
- ½ cup quick-cooking barley   100 g
- 1 (15 ounce) can Italian stewed tomatoes   425 g

Combine beans, onion, celery, broth, barley, stewed tomatoes and ½ teaspoon (2 ml) pepper in sprayed 6-quart (6 L) slow cooker and stir well.

Cover and cook on LOW for 4 to 5 hours. Serves 6 to 8.

> When you want to adapt a recipe for the slow cooker, it is best to reduce the liquid unless rice or pasta is used. The slow cooker itself makes some liquid through condensation and the ingredients sometimes make more liquid. If you are using rice or pasta, 1 cup (250 ml) liquid will usually be correct.

47

Pinto Bean-Vegetable Soup

- 4 (15 ounce) cans seasoned pinto beans with liquid   4 (425 g)
- 1 (10 ounce) package frozen seasoning blend (chopped onions and bell peppers)   280 g
- 2 cups chopped celery   200 g
- 2 (14 ounce) cans chicken broth   2 (395 g)
- 1 teaspoon Cajun seasoning   5 ml
- ⅛ teaspoon cayenne pepper   .5 ml

Place all ingredients plus 1 cup (250 ml) water in sprayed 5-quart (5 L) slow cooker and stir well.

Cover and cook on LOW 5 to 6 hours. Serves 6 to 8.

Tasty Chicken and Rice Soup

- 1 pound boneless, skinless chicken breasts   455 g
- ½ cup brown rice   95 g
- 1 (10 ounce) can cream of chicken soup   280 g
- 1 (10 ounce) can cream of celery soup   280 g
- 1 (14 ounce) can chicken broth with roasted garlic   395 g
- 1 (16 ounce) package frozen sliced carrots, thawed   455 g
- 1 cup half-and-half cream   250 ml

Cut chicken into 1-inch pieces. Place pieces in sprayed 4 to 5-quart (4 to 5 L) slow cooker.

Combine and mix rice, soups, chicken broth and carrots in bowl and pour over chicken. Cover and cook on LOW 7 to 8 hours.

Turn heat to HIGH, add half-and-half cream and cook for additional 15 to 20 minutes. Serves 6 to 8.

As with any recipe, read the entire recipe before you begin preparing food for the slow cooker.

Confetti Chicken Soup

• 1 pound boneless, skinless chicken thighs	455 g
• 1 (6 ounce) package chicken and herb-flavored rice	170 g
• 3 (14 ounce) cans chicken broth	3 (395 g)
• 3 carrots, sliced	
• 1 (10 ounce) can cream of chicken soup	280 g
• 1½ tablespoons chicken seasoning	22 ml
• 1 (10 ounce) package frozen whole kernel corn, thawed	280 g
• 1 (10 ounce) package frozen baby green peas, thawed	280 g

Cut thighs in thin strips. Combine chicken, rice, chicken broth, carrots, soup, seasoning and 1 cup (250 ml) water in sprayed 5 to 6-quart (5 to 6 L) slow cooker.

Cover and cook on LOW for 8 to 9 hours.

About 30 minutes before serving, turn heat to HIGH and add corn and peas to cooker. Continue cooking for additional 30 minutes. Serves 4 to 6.

Veggie Medley Soup

• 2 (15 ounce) cans Mexican stewed tomatoes	2 (425 g)
• 2 (14 ounce) cans chicken broth	2 (395 g)
• 2 (10 ounce) cans chicken noodle soup	2 (280 g)
• 1 (15 ounce) can shoe-peg corn or white corn, drained	425 g
• 1 (15 ounce) can cut green beans, drained	425 g
• Shredded pepper-Jack cheese	

Place all ingredients except cheese in sprayed 4 to 5-quart (4 to 5 L) slow cooker and mix well.

Cover and cook on LOW for 2 to 3 hours. When ready to serve, sprinkle shredded cheese over each bowl of soup. Serves 4 to 6.

Do not use meats that are still frozen because they may not cook thoroughly; this is not a problem with frozen vegetables.

Chicken-Vegetable Soup

- 1½ pounds boneless, skinless chicken thighs, cubed   680 g
- 1 onion, chopped
- 3 carrots, sliced
- ½ cup halved, pitted ripe olives   65 g
- 1 teaspoon minced garlic   5 ml
- 3 (14 ounce) cans chicken broth   3 (395 g)
- 1 (15 ounce) can Italian stewed tomatoes   425 g
- 1 teaspoon Italian seasoning   5 ml
- ½ cup small shell pasta   55 g
- Parmesan cheese

Combine all ingredients except shell pasta and parmesan cheese in sprayed slow cooker.

Cover and cook on LOW for 8 to 9 hours. About 30 minutes before serving, add pasta and stir.

Increase heat to HIGH and cook for additional 20 to 30 minutes. Garnish with parmesan cheese. Serves 6 to 8.

Chicken and Rice Soup

• 1 (6 ounce) package long grain-wild rice mix	170 g
• 1 (1 ounce) packet chicken noodle soup mix	30 g
• 2 (10 ounce) cans cream of chicken soup	2 (280 g)
• 2 ribs celery, chopped	
• 1 - 2 cups cooked, cubed chicken	140 - 280 g

Combine rice mix, noodle soup mix, chicken soup, celery, chicken and about 6 cups (1.4 L) water in sprayed 5 to 6-quart (5 to 6 L) slow cooker.

Cover and cook on LOW for 2 to 3 hours. Serves 4 to 6.

Chicken and Barley Soup

• 1½ - 2 pounds boneless, skinless chicken thighs	680 - 910 g
• 1 (16 ounce) package frozen stew vegetables	455 g
• 1 (1 ounce) packet dry vegetable soup mix	30 g
• 1¼ cups pearl barley	250 g
• 2 (14 ounce) cans chicken broth	2 (395 g)
• 1 teaspoon white pepper	5 ml

Combine all ingredients with 1 teaspoon (5 ml) salt and 4 cups (1 L) water in sprayed, large slow cooker.

Cover and cook on LOW for 5 to 6 hours or on HIGH for 3 hours. Serves 6 to 8.

Mild Vegetarian Chili

- 3 (15 ounce) cans navy beans with liquid   3 (425 g)
- 3 (14 ounce) cans chicken broth   3 (395 g)
- 1 (10 ounce) can cream of chicken soup   280 g
- 2 tablespoons butter, melted   28 g
- 2 onions, chopped
- 3 cups cooked, chopped chicken or turkey   420 g
- 1 (7 ounce) can chopped green chilies   200 g
- 1 teaspoon minced garlic   5 ml
- ½ teaspoon dried basil   2 ml
- ⅛ teaspoon cayenne pepper   .5 ml
- ⅛ teaspoon ground cloves   .5 ml
- 1 teaspoon ground oregano   5 ml
- 1 (8 ounce) package shredded 4-cheese blend   225 g

Combine all ingredients except cheese in sprayed slow cooker. Cover and cook on LOW for 4 to 5 hours.

When serving, sprinkle cheese over top of each serving. Serves 6 to 8.

Tortilla Soup

- **3 large boneless, skinless chicken breast halves, cubed**
- **1 (10 ounce) package frozen whole kernel corn, thawed**   **280 g**
- **1 onion, chopped**
- **3 (14 ounce) cans chicken broth**   **3 (395 g)**
- **1 (6 ounce) can tomato paste**   **170 g**
- **2 (10 ounce) cans tomatoes and green chilies**   **2 (280 g)**
- **2 teaspoons ground cumin**   **10 ml**
- **1 teaspoon chili powder**   **5 ml**
- **1 teaspoon minced garlic**   **5 ml**
- **6 corn tortillas**

Combine chicken cubes, corn, onion, broth, tomato paste, tomatoes and green chilies, cumin, chili powder, 1 teaspoon (5 ml) salt and garlic in sprayed, large slow cooker.

Cover and cook on LOW for 5 to 7 hours or on HIGH for 3 hours to 3 hours 30 minutes.

Preheat oven to 375° (190° C).

While soup is cooking, cut tortillas into ¼-inch (6 mm) strips and place on baking sheet. Bake for about 5 minutes or until crisp.

Serve baked tortilla strips with soup. Serves 6 to 8.

Turkey-Veggie Chili

• 1 pound ground turkey	455 g
• Canola oil	
• 2 (15 ounce) cans pinto beans with liquid	2 (425 g)
• 1 (15 ounce) can great northern beans with liquid	425 g
• 1 (14 ounce) can chicken broth	395 g
• 2 (15 ounce) cans Mexican stewed tomatoes	2 (425 g)
• 1 (8 ounce) can whole kernel corn	225 g
• 1 large onion, chopped	
• 1 red bell pepper, chopped	
• 2 teaspoons minced garlic	10 ml
• 2 teaspoons ground cumin	10 ml
• ½ cup elbow macaroni	55 g
• Sour cream or shredded cheddar cheese	

Cook and brown turkey in skillet with a little oil before placing in sprayed, large slow cooker.

Add beans, broth, tomatoes, corn, onion, bell pepper, garlic, cumin and a little salt and stir well.

Cover and cook on LOW for 4 to 5 hours.

Stir in macaroni and continue cooking for about 15 minutes. Stir to make sure macaroni does not stick to cooker and cook for additional 15 minutes or until macaroni is tender. Serves 6 to 8.

TIP: Top each serving with dab of sour cream or 1 tablespoon (15 ml) shredded cheddar cheese.

Turkey and Mushroom Soup

Another great way to use leftover chicken or turkey

• 2 cups sliced shitake mushrooms	145 g
• 2 ribs celery, sliced	
• 1 small onion, chopped	
• 2 tablespoons butter	30 g
• 1 (15 ounce) can sliced carrots	425 g
• 2 (14 ounce) cans chicken broth	395 g
• ½ cup orzo pasta	40 g
• 2 cups cooked, chopped turkey	280 g

Saute mushrooms, celery and onion in butter in skillet. Transfer vegetables to sprayed slow cooker and add carrots, broth, orzo and turkey. (Do not use smoked turkey.)

Cover and cook on LOW for 2 to 3 hours or on HIGH for 1 to 2 hours. Serves 4 to 6.

Turkey-Tortilla Soup

This is great for leftover turkey.

• 2 (14 ounce) cans chicken broth	2 (395 g)
• 2 (15 ounce) cans Mexican stewed tomatoes	2 (425 g)
• 1 (16 ounce) package frozen succotash, thawed	455 g
• 2 teaspoons chili powder	10 ml
• 1 teaspoon dried cilantro	5 ml
• 2 cups crushed tortilla chips, divided	110 g
• 2½ cups cooked, chopped turkey	350 g

Combine broth, tomatoes, succotash, chili powder, cilantro, ⅓ cup (20 g) crushed tortilla chips and turkey in sprayed, large slow cooker and stir well.

Cover and cook on LOW for 3 to 5 hours. When ready to serve, sprinkle remaining chips over each serving. Serves 6 to 8.

TIP: Do not use smoked turkey.

2-Sausage Meatball Soup

- 1 pound mild bulk Italian sausage — 455 g
- 1 pound hot bulk pork sausage — 455 g
- 2 (15 ounce) cans Mexican stewed tomatoes — 2 (425 g)
- 1 onion, chopped
- 3 cups chopped celery — 305 g
- 1 cup sliced carrots — 120 g
- 1 (15 ounce) can cut green beans, drained — 425 g
- 1 (14 ounce) can chicken broth — 395 g
- 1 teaspoon seasoned salt — 5 ml

Combine mild and hot sausage, shape into small balls and place in non-stick skillet. Brown thoroughly and drain.

Place in sprayed, large slow cooker. Add remaining ingredients plus 1 cup (250 ml) water and stir gently so meatballs will not break-up.

Cover and cook on LOW 6 to 7 hours. Serves 6 to 8.

Mexican-Meatball Soup

- 3 (14 ounce) cans beef broth — 3 (395 g)
- 1 (16 ounce) jar hot salsa — 455 g
- 1 (16 ounce) package frozen whole kernel corn, thawed — 455 g
- 1 (16 ounce) package frozen meatballs, thawed — 455 g
- 1 teaspoon minced garlic — 5 ml

Combine all ingredients in sprayed, slow cooker and stir well. Cover and cook on LOW for 5 to 7 hours. Serves 6 to 8.

Chicken thighs are more flavorful and less likely to overcook than chicken breasts in slow cooker recipes.

Taco Soup Olé

- **2 pounds lean ground beef** — 910 g
- **2 (15 ounce) cans ranch-style beans with liquid** — 2 (425 g)
- **1 (15 ounce) can whole kernel corn, drained** — 425 g
- **2 (15 ounce) cans stewed tomatoes** — 2 (425 g)
- **1 (10 ounce) can diced tomatoes and green chilies** — 280 g
- **1 (.04 ounce) packet ranch dressing mix** — 10 g
- **1 (1 ounce) packet taco seasoning** — 30 g
- **Shredded cheddar cheese**

Brown ground beef in large skillet, drain and transfer to sprayed slow cooker. Add remaining ingredients and stir well.

Cover and cook on LOW for 8 to 10 hours. When serving, sprinkle cheese over each serving. Serve 6 to 8.

Tasty Cabbage and Beef Soup

- **1 pound lean ground beef** — 455 g
- **1 (16 ounce) package coleslaw mix** — 455 g
- **1 (15 ounce) can cut green beans** — 425 g
- **1 (15 ounce) can whole kernel corn** — 425 g
- **2 (15 ounce) cans Italian stewed tomatoes** — 2 (425 g)
- **2 (14 ounce) cans beef broth** — 2 (395 g)
- **Cornbread**

Brown ground beef in skillet, drain and place in sprayed, large slow cooker. Add slaw mix, green beans, corn, tomatoes and beef broth and add a little salt and pepper.

Cover and cook on LOW for 7 to 9 hours. Serve with cornbread. Serves 6 to 8.

> *Large or firm vegetables like potatoes, onions and carrots cook more slowly than meat. Put these vegetables in the slow cooker first and put the meat on top of them.*

Taco Soup

- **1½ pounds lean ground beef**   **680 g**
- **1 (1 ounce) packet taco seasoning**   **30 g**
- **2 (15 ounce) cans Mexican stewed tomatoes**   **2 (425 g)**
- **2 (15 ounce) cans chili beans with liquid**   **2 (425 g)**
- **1 (15 ounce) can whole kernel corn, drained**   **425 g**
- **Crushed tortilla chips**
- **Shredded cheddar cheese**

Brown ground beef in skillet until it is no longer pink. Place in sprayed 5 to 6-quart (5 to 6 L) slow cooker.

Add taco seasoning, tomatoes, chili beans, corn and 1 cup (250 ml) water and mix well.

Cover and cook on LOW for 4 hours or on HIGH for 1 to 2 hours.

Serve over crushed tortilla chips and sprinkle some shredded cheddar cheese over top of each serving. Serves 6 to 8.

Easy-Fix Meatball Soup

• 1 (32 ounce) package frozen meatballs, thawed	1 kg
• 2 (15 ounce) cans stewed tomatoes	2 (425 g)
• 3 large potatoes, peeled, diced	
• 4 carrots, peeled, sliced	
• 2 medium onions, chopped	
• 2 (14 ounce) cans beef broth	2 (395 g)
• 2 tablespoons cornstarch	15 g

Combine meatballs, tomatoes, potatoes, carrots, onions, beef broth, a little salt and pepper and 1 cup (250 ml) water in sprayed 6-quart (6 L) slow cooker.

Cover and cook on LOW for 5 to 6 hours.

Turn heat to HIGH and combine cornstarch with ¼ cup (60 ml) water in bowl. Pour into cooker and cook for additional 10 or 15 minutes or until slightly thick. Serves 4 to 6.

Hamburger-Chili Mix

• 2 pounds lean ground beef	910 g
• 2 (15 ounce) cans chili without beans	2 (425 g)
• 1 (16 ounce) package frozen mixed vegetables, thawed	455 g
• 3 (14 ounce) cans beef broth	3 (395 g)
• 2 (15 ounce) cans stewed tomatoes	2 (425 g)
• 1 teaspoon seasoned salt	5 ml

Brown ground beef in skillet until no longer pink. Place in sprayed 6-quart (6 L) slow cooker.

Add chili, vegetables, broth, tomatoes, 1 cup (250 ml) water and seasoned salt and stir well. Cover and cook on LOW for 6 to 7 hours. Serves 6 to 8.

Enchilada Soup

- 1 pound lean ground beef, browned, drained   455 g
- 1 (15 ounce) can Mexican stewed tomatoes   425 g
- 1 (15 ounce) can pinto beans with liquid   425 g
- 1 (15 ounce) can whole kernel corn with liquid   425 g
- 1 onion, chopped
- 2 (10 ounce) cans enchilada sauce   2 (280 g)
- 1 (8 ounce) package shredded 4-cheese blend   225 g
- Tortilla chips

Combine beef, tomatoes, beans, corn, onion, enchilada sauce and 1 cup (250 ml) water in sprayed 5 to 6-quart (5 to 6 L) slow cooker and mix well.

Cover and cook on LOW for 6 to 8 hours or on HIGH for 3 to 4 hours.

Stir in shredded cheese. If desired, top each serving with a few crushed tortilla chips. Serves 6 to 8.

Mexican Tomato-Chili Soup

- 3 (15 ounce) cans chili with beans   3 (425 g)
- 1 (15 ounce) can whole kernel corn   425 g
- 1 (14 ounce) can beef broth   395 g
- 2 (15 ounce) cans Mexican stewed tomatoes   2 (425 g)
- 2 teaspoons ground cumin   10 ml
- 2 teaspoons chili powder   10 ml
- Flour tortillas

Combine chili, corn, broth, tomatoes, cumin, chili powder and 1 cup (250 ml) water in sprayed 5 to 6-quart (5 to 6 L) slow cooker.

Cover and cook on LOW for 4 to 5 hours. Serve with warm, buttered flour tortillas. Serves 6 to 8.

Beefy Black Bean-Tomato Soup

- 1 pound lean ground beef   455 g
- 2 onions, chopped
- 2 cups sliced celery   200 g
- 1 onion, chopped
- 2 (14 ounce) cans beef broth   2 (395 g)
- 1 (15 ounce) can Mexican stewed tomatoes   425 g
- 2 (15 ounce) cans black beans, rinsed, drained   2 (425 g)

Brown beef in skillet until no longer pink. Place in sprayed 5 to 6-quart (5 to 6 L) slow cooker.

Add onions, celery, onion, broth, tomatoes, black beans, ¾ cup (175 ml) water plus a little salt and pepper.

Cover and cook on LOW for 6 to 7 hours or on HIGH for 3 hours to 3 hours 30 minutes. Serves 6 to 8.

TIP: If you like a zestier soup, add 1 teaspoon (5 ml) chili powder.

Beef and Noodle Soup

- 1½ pounds lean ground beef   680 g
- 1 onion, chopped
- 2 (15 ounce) cans mixed vegetables, drained   2 (425 g)
- 2 (15 ounce) cans Italian stewed tomatoes   2 (425 g)
- 2 (14 ounce) cans beef broth   2 (395 g)
- 1 teaspoon dried oregano   5 ml
- 1 cup medium egg noodles   75 g

Brown and cook ground beef in skillet until no longer pink and transfer to sprayed slow cooker.

Add onion, mixed vegetables, stewed tomatoes, beef broth and oregano.

Cover and cook on LOW for 4 to 5 hours.

Cook noodles according to package direction. Add noodles to slow cooker and cook for additional 30 minutes. Serves 4 to 6.

Beef and Barley Soup

- 1 pound lean ground beef   455 g
- 3 (14 ounce) cans beef broth   3 (395 g)
- ¾ cup quick-cooking barley   150 g
- 3 cups sliced carrots   365 g
- 2 cups sliced celery   200 g
- 2 teaspoons beef seasoning   10 ml

Brown ground beef in skillet, drain and transfer to sprayed 5-quart (5 L) slow cooker.

Add beef broth, barley, carrots, celery and beef seasoning. Cover and cook on LOW for 7 to 8 hours. Serves 4.

Grandma's Hominy Soup

- 2 pounds pork shoulder   910 g
- 1 onion, chopped
- 2 ribs celery, sliced
- 2 (15 ounce) cans yellow hominy with liquid   2 (425 g)
- 2 (15 ounce) cans stewed tomatoes   2 (425 g)
- 2 (14 ounce) cans chicken broth   2 (395 g)
- 1½ teaspoons ground cumin   7 ml

Cut pork into ½-inch (1.2 cm) cubes. Sprinkle pork cubes with a little salt and pepper and brown in skillet. Place in sprayed slow cooker.

Combine onion, celery, hominy, stewed tomatoes, cumin and 1 cup (250 ml) water in bowl. Pour over pork cubes.

Cover and cook on HIGH for 6 to 7 hours.

Serve with cornbread or white bread. Serves 6 to 8.

Ham, Bean and Pasta Soup

- 1 onion, finely chopped
- 2 ribs celery, chopped
- 2 teaspoons minced garlic   10 ml
- 2 (14 ounce) cans chicken broth   2 (395 g)
- 2 (15 ounce) cans pork and beans with liquid   2 (425 g)
- 3 cups cooked, cubed ham   420 g
- ⅓ cup pasta shells   35 g
- Bacon, cooked

Combine onion, celery, garlic, chicken broth, beans, ham and 1 cup (250 ml) water in sprayed 5 to 6-quart (5 to 6 L) slow cooker.

Cover and cook on LOW for 4 to 5 hours.

Turn cooker to HIGH heat, add pasta and cook for additional 35 to 45 minutes or until pasta is tender.

Garnish each serving with cooked, crisp and crumbled bacon. Serves 6 to 8.

Sausage-Pizza Soup

- 1 (16 ounce) package Italian link sausage, thinly sliced   455 g
- 1 onion, chopped
- 2 (4 ounce) cans sliced mushrooms   2 (115 g)
- 1 small green bell pepper, cored, seeded, julienned
- 1 (15 ounce) can Italian stewed tomatoes   425 g
- 1 (14 ounce) can beef broth   395 g
- 1 (8 ounce) can pizza sauce   225 g
- Shredded mozzarella cheese

Combine all ingredients except cheese in sprayed slow cooker and stir well.

Cover and cook on LOW for 4 to 5 hours.

Sprinkle mozzarella cheese over each serving. Serves 4 to 6.

Southern Ham Stew

This is great served with cornbread.

- **2 cups dried black-eyed peas** — 480 g
- **3 cups cooked, cubed ham** — 420 g
- **1 large onion, chopped**
- **2 cups sliced celery** — 200 g
- **1 (15 ounce) can yellow hominy, drained** — 425 g
- **2 (15 ounce) cans stewed tomatoes** — 2 (425 g)
- **1 (10 ounce) can chicken broth** — 280 g
- **2 teaspoons seasoned salt** — 10 ml
- **2 tablespoons cornstarch** — 15 g

Rinse and drain dried black-eyed peas in saucepan. Cover peas with water, bring to a boil and drain again.

Place peas in sprayed, large slow cooker and add 5 cups (1.2 L) water, ham, onion, celery, hominy, tomatoes, broth and seasoned salt.

Cover and cook on LOW for 7 to 9 hours. Mix cornstarch with ⅓ cup (75 ml) water in bowl, turn cooker to HIGH heat, pour in cornstarch mixture and stir well.

Cook for about 10 minutes or until stew thickens. Serves 6 to 8.

TIP: If you would like a little spice in the stew, substitute one of the cans of stewed tomatoes with the Mexican stewed tomatoes.

Pork Tenderloin-Rice Stew

- **1 (2 pound) pork tenderloin**   **910 g**
- **1 onion, coarsely chopped**
- **1 red bell pepper, seeded, sliced**
- **1 (16 ounce) package frozen mixed vegetables, thawed**   **455 g**
- **2 tablespoons flour**   **15 g**
- **½ teaspoon dried rosemary leaves**   **2 ml**
- **½ teaspoon oregano leaves**   **2 ml**
- **1 (10 ounce) can chicken broth**   **280 g**
- **1 (6 ounce) package long grain-wild rice**   **170 g**

Cut tenderloin into 1-inch (2.5 cm) cubes. Brown tenderloin cubes in non-stick skillet and place in sprayed, large slow cooker.

Add onion, bell pepper and mixed vegetables. Combine flour, rosemary and oregano into chicken broth in bowl and pour over vegetables.

Cover and cook on LOW for 4 hours to 4 hours 30 minutes.

When ready to serve, cook rice according to package directions. Serve pork and vegetables over rice. Serves 4 to 6.

Ham and Cabbage Stew

- **2 (15 ounce) can Italian stewed tomatoes**   2 (425 g)
- **3 cups shredded cabbage**   210 g
- **1 onion, chopped**
- **1 red bell pepper, cored, seeded, chopped**
- **2 tablespoons butter, sliced**   30 g
- **1 (14 ounce) can chicken broth**   395 g
- **¾ teaspoon seasoned salt**   4 ml
- **3 cups cooked, diced ham**   420 g
- **Cornbread**

Combine all ingredients with ¾ teaspoons (4 ml) pepper and 1 cup (250 ml) water in sprayed, large slow cooker and stir to mix well.

Cover and cook on LOW for 5 to 7 hours. Serve with cornbread. Serves 4 to 6.

Southern Ham and Black-eyed Peas

- **1½ cups dried black-eyed peas**   360 g
- **2 - 3 cups cooked, cubed ham**   280 - 420 g
- **1 (15 ounce) can whole kernel corn**   425 g
- **1 (10 ounce) package frozen cut okra, thawed**   280 g
- **1 onion, chopped**
- **1 large potato, cubed**
- **2 teaspoons Cajun seasoning**   10 ml
- **1 (14 ounce) can chicken broth**   395 g
- **2 (15 ounce) cans Mexican stewed tomatoes**   2 (425 g)

Rinse peas and drain. Combine peas and 5 cups (1.2 L) water in large saucepan. Bring to a boil, reduce heat, simmer for about 10 minutes and drain.

Combine peas, ham, corn, okra, onion, potato, seasoning, broth and 2 cups (500 ml) water in sprayed 5 to 6-quart (5 to 6 L) slow cooker. Cover and cook on LOW for 6 to 8 hours.

Add stewed tomatoes and continue cooking for additional 1 hour. Serves 6 to 8.

Beans 'n Sausage Soup

- **1 pound hot Italian sausage**   **455 g**
- **1 onion, chopped**
- **1 (15 ounce) can Italian stewed tomatoes**   **425 g**
- **2 (5 ounce) cans black beans, rinsed, drained**   **2 (145 g)**
- **2 (15 ounce) cans navy beans with liquid**   **2 (425 g)**
- **2 (14 ounce) cans beef broth**   **2 (395 g)**
- **1 teaspoon minced garlic**   **5 ml**
- **1 teaspoon dried basil**   **5 ml**

Cut sausage into ½-inch (1.2 cm) pieces. Brown sausage and onion in skillet, drain and transfer to sprayed 5 to 6-quart (5 to 6 L) slow cooker.

Stir in tomatoes, black beans, navy beans, broth, garlic and basil and mix well. Cover and cook on LOW for 5 to 7 hours. Serves 6 to 8.

Recipes in this cookbook may be cooked in 3 to 6-quart slow cookers. You may need to adjust the quantity of ingredients for a smaller cooker.

Chicken Stew over Biscuits

- **2 (1 ounce) packets chicken gravy mix** — 2 (30 g)
- **2 cups sliced celery** — 200 g
- **1 (10 ounce) package frozen sliced carrots** — 280 g
- **1 (10 ounce) package frozen green peas, thawed** — 280 g
- **1 teaspoon dried basil** — 5 ml
- **3 cups cooked, cubed chicken** — 280 g
- **Buttermilk biscuits**

Combine gravy mix, 2 cups (500 ml) water, celery, carrots, peas, basil, ¾ teaspoon (4 ml) each of salt and pepper and chicken in sprayed slow cooker.

Cover and cook on LOW for 6 to 7 hours. Serve over baked refrigerated buttermilk biscuits. Serves 4 to 6.

TIP: If you like thick stew, mix 2 tablespoons (15 g) cornstarch with ¼ cup (60 ml) water and stir into chicken mixture. Cook for additional 30 minutes to thicken.

Chicken-Tortellini Stew

- **1 (9 ounce) package refrigerated cheese-filled tortellini** — 255 g
- **2 medium yellow squash, halved, sliced**
- **1 red bell pepper, seeded, coarsely chopped**
- **1 onion, chopped**
- **2 (14 ounce) cans chicken broth** — 2 (395 g)
- **1 teaspoon dried rosemary** — 5 ml
- **½ teaspoon dried basil** — 2 ml
- **2 cups cooked, chopped chicken** — 280 g

Place tortellini, squash, bell pepper and onion in sprayed slow cooker. Stir in broth, rosemary, basil and chicken.

Cover and cook on LOW for 2 to 4 hours or until tortellini and vegetables are tender. Serves 4.

Chicken Stew

- 4 large boneless, skinless chicken breast halves, cubed
- 3 medium potatoes, peeled, cubed
- 1 (26 ounce) jar meatless spaghetti sauce   740 g
- 1 (15 ounce) can cut green beans, drained   425 g
- 1 (15 ounce) can whole kernel corn   425 g
- 1 tablespoon chicken seasoning   15 ml

Combine chicken, potatoes, spaghetti sauce, green beans, corn, chicken seasoning and ¾ cup (175 ml) water in sprayed 5 to 6-quart (5 to 6 L) slow cooker.

Cover and cook on LOW for 6 to 7 hours. Serves 4 to 6.

Black-Northern-Pinto Bean Stew

- 1 (16 ounce) package smoked sausage links   455 g
- 1 (28 ounce) can baked beans with liquid   795 g
- 1 (15 ounce) can great northern beans with liquid   425 g
- 1 (15 ounce) can pinto beans with liquid   425 g
- 1 (15 ounce) can lentil soup   425 g
- 1 onion, chopped
- 1 teaspoon Cajun seasoning   5 ml
- 2 (15 ounce) cans stewed tomatoes   2 (425 g)
- Corn muffins

Peel skin from sausage links and slice. Place in sprayed 6-quart (6 L) slow cooker, add remaining ingredients and stir to mix.

Cover and cook on LOW for 3 to 4 hours. Serve with corn muffins. Serves 6 to 8.

Beefy Stew with Rice

- **1 pound lean beef stew meat**   **455 g**
- **1 (14 ounce) can beef broth**   **395 g**
- **1 (7 ounce) box beef-flavored rice and vermicelli mix**   **200 g**
- **1 (10 ounce) package frozen peas and carrots**   **280 g**
- **2½ cups vegetable juice**   **625 ml**

Sprinkle stew meat with seasoned pepper, brown in non-stick skillet, drain and place in sprayed, large slow cooker.

Add broth, rice and vermicelli mix, peas and carrots, vegetable juice and 2 cups (500 ml) water.

Cover and cook on LOW for 6 to 7 hours. Serves 4 to 6.

Apple Cider Stew

- **1 pound cubed beef stew meat**   **455 g**
- **3 cups apple cider**   **750 ml**
- **2 tablespoons cider vinegar**   **30 ml**
- **10 small red potatoes, halved**
- **½ (12 ounce) package baby carrots**   **½ (340 g)**
- **2 apples with peels, cored, sliced**

Dredge stew meat through a little flour and brown on all sides in skillet with a little oil. Pour into sprayed slow cooker.

Pour apple cider and vinegar into slow cooker and stir. Place all ingredients into slow cooker with beef on top. Cook on LOW for 8 to 10 hours or until meat is tender. Serves 4.

Slow cookers aren't just for cooking when it's cold and wintry outside. It's also great to use in the summer so you don't heat up the kitchen with the oven and you use much less energy with the slow cooker than the oven.

Oriental Beef Stew

- **2 pounds premium lean beef stew meat** — 910 g
- **1 (16 ounce) package frozen Oriental stir-fry vegetables, thawed** — 455 g
- **1 (10 ounce) can beefy mushroom soup** — 280 g
- **1 (10 ounce) can beef broth** — 280 g
- **⅔ cup bottled sweet-and-sour sauce** — 150 ml
- **1 tablespoon beef seasoning** — 15 ml

Brown stew meat sprinkled with ½ teaspoon (2 ml) pepper in skillet and place in sprayed slow cooker.

Combine vegetables, soup, broth, sweet-and-sour sauce, beef seasoning and 1 cup (250 ml) water in bowl. Pour over stew meat and stir well.

Cover and cook on LOW for 5 to 7 hours. Serves 4 to 6.

Santa Fe Stew

A hearty, filling soup.

- **1½ pounds lean ground beef** — 680 g
- **1 (14 ounce) can beef broth** — 395 g
- **1 (15 ounce) can whole kernel corn with liquid** — 425 g
- **2 (15 ounce) cans pinto beans with liquid** — 2 (425 g)
- **2 (15 ounce) cans Mexican stewed tomatoes** — 2 (425 g)
- **1 teaspoon beef seasoning** — 5 ml
- **1 (16 ounce) package cubed Velveeta® cheese** — 455 g

Brown beef in skillet until no longer pink.

Place in sprayed 5 to 6-quart (5 to 6 L) slow cooker and add broth, corn, beans, tomatoes and beef seasoning.

Cover and cook on LOW for 5 to 6 hours.

When ready to serve, fold in cheese and stir until cheese melts. Serves 6 to 8.

TIP: Cornbread is a must to serve with this stew.

Taco-Chili Stew

- **2 pounds very lean stew meat**   **910 g**
- **2 (15 ounce) cans Mexican stewed tomatoes**   **2 (425 g)**
- **1 (1 ounce) packet taco seasoning mix**   **30 g**
- **2 (15 ounce) cans pinto beans with liquid**   **2 (425 g)**
- **1 (15 ounce) can whole kernel corn with liquid**   **425 g**
- **Green onions, chopped**

Cut large pieces of stew meat in half and brown in large skillet.

Combine stew meat, tomatoes, taco seasoning mix, beans, corn and ¾ cup (175 ml) water in sprayed 4 to 5-quart (4 to 5 L) slow cooker. (If you are not into "spicy", use original recipe stewed tomatoes instead of Mexican.)

Cover and cook on LOW for 5 to 7 hours. Garnish each serving with chopped green onions. Serves 6 to 8.

Cooking time on HIGH equals about half the cooking time on LOW.

Pancho Villa Stew

- **3 cups cooked, diced ham** — **420 g**
- **1 pound smoked sausage** — **455 g**
- **3 (14 ounce) cans chicken broth** — **3 (395 g)**
- **1 (15 ounce) can diced tomatoes** — **425 g**
- **1 (7 ounce) can chopped green chilies** — **200 g**
- **1 onion, chopped**
- **2 (15 ounce) cans pinto beans with liquid** — **2 (425 g)**
- **1 (15 ounce) can whole kernel corn** — **425 g**
- **1 teaspoon garlic powder** — **5 ml**
- **2 teaspoons ground cumin** — **10 ml**
- **2 teaspoons cocoa** — **10 ml**
- **1 teaspoon dried oregano** — **5 ml**
- **Flour tortillas**

Cut sausage into ½-inch (1.2 cm) pieces.

Combine all ingredients and 1 teaspoon (5 ml) salt except tortillas in sprayed slow cooker and stir well.

Cover and cook on LOW for 5 to 7 hours.

Serve with buttered, flour tortillas. Serves 6 to 8.

73

Mixed Vegetable Beef Stew

- **3 cups leftover roast beef, cubed**   **420 g**
- **1 onion, chopped**
- **2 ribs celery, chopped**
- **2 (15 ounce) cans stewed tomatoes**   **2 (425 g)**
- **1 (16 ounce) package frozen mixed vegetables, thawed**   **455 g**
- **2 (14 ounce) cans beef broth**   **2 (395 g)**
- **1 cup cauliflower florets**   **100 g**
- **1 cup broccoli florets**   **70 g**

Combine all ingredients except cauliflower and broccoli in sprayed 6-quart (6 L) slow cooker. Add a little salt and pepper.

Cover and cook on LOW for 3 to 4 hours.

Stir in cauliflower and broccoli and continue cooking for additional 2 hours until tender. Serves 6 to 8.

Meaty Potato Stew with Tortillas

- **1½ - 2 pounds lean beef stew meat**   **680 - 910 g**
- **2 (15 ounce) cans pinto beans with liquid**   **2 (425 g)**
- **1 onion, chopped**
- **3 carrots, sliced**
- **2 medium potatoes, cubed**
- **1 (1 ounce) packet taco seasoning**   **30 g**
- **2 (15 ounce) cans Mexican stewed tomatoes**   **2 (425 g)**
- **Flour tortillas**

Brown stew meat in non-stick skillet. Combine meat, pinto beans, onion, carrots, potatoes, taco seasoning and 2 cups (500 ml) water in sprayed, large slow cooker.

Cover and cook on LOW for 6 to 7 hours. Add stewed tomatoes and cook for additional 1 hour. This is great served with warmed, buttered, flour tortillas. Serves 4 to 6.

Vegetable-Beef Stew

- **1 (18 ounce) package frozen cooked meatballs, thawed**   **510 g**
- **1 (16 ounce) package frozen mixed vegetables**   **455 g**
- **1 (15 ounce) can stewed tomatoes**   **425 g**
- **1 (12 ounce) jar beef gravy**   **340 g**
- **2 teaspoons crushed dried basil**   **10 ml**

Place meatballs and mixed vegetables in sprayed slow cooker. Combine stewed tomatoes, gravy, basil, ½ teaspoon (2 ml) black pepper and ½ cup (125 ml) water in bowl and stir.

Pour over meatballs and vegetables. Cover and cook on LOW for 6 to 7 hours. Serves 4 to 6.

Can Opener Meatball Stew

- **1 (18 ounce) package frozen prepared Italian meatballs, thawed**   **510 g**
- **1 (14 ounce) can beef broth**   **395 g**
- **1 (15 ounce) can cut green beans**   **425 g**
- **1 (16 ounce) package baby carrots**   **455 g**
- **2 (15 ounce) cans stewed tomatoes**   **2 (425 g)**
- **1 tablespoon Worcestershire sauce**   **15 ml**

Combine all ingredients in sprayed slow cooker. Cover and cook on LOW for 3 to 5 hours. Serves 4 to 6.

Italian-Vegetable Stew

- 1½ - 2 pounds Italian sausage — 680 - 910 g
- 2 (16 ounce) packages frozen vegetables — 2 (455 g)
- 2 (15 ounce) cans Italian stewed tomatoes — 2 (425 g)
- 1 (14 ounce) can beef broth — 395 g
- 1 teaspoon Italian seasoning — 5 ml
- ½ cup pasta shells — 55 g

Brown sausage and cook in skillet for about 5 minutes and drain.

Combine sausage, vegetables, stewed tomatoes, broth, Italian seasoning and shells in sprayed 5 to 6-quart (5 to 6 L) slow cooker and mix well.

Cover and cook on LOW for 3 to 5 hours. Serves 4 to 6.

Hungarian Stew

- 2 pounds boneless short ribs — 910 g
- 1 cup pearl barley — 200 g
- 1 small onion, chopped
- 1 green bell pepper, cored, seeded, chopped
- 1 teaspoon minced garlic — 5 ml
- 2 (15 ounce) cans kidney beans, drained — 2 (425 g)
- 2 (14 ounce) cans beef broth — 2 (395 g)
- 1 tablespoon paprika — 15 ml

Combine all ingredients plus 1 cup (250 ml) water in sprayed slow cooker.

Cover and cook on LOW for 8 to 9 hours or on HIGH for 4 hours 30 minutes to 5 hours. Serves 4 to 6.

Dried beans need to be soft before they are added to the slow cooker to cook. Be sure to soak beans overnight or soak for 1 hour and boil for about 10 minutes before cooking in slow cooker.

Hearty Meatball Stew

• 1 (28 ounce) package frozen meatballs, thawed	795 g
• 2 (15 ounce) cans Italian stewed tomatoes	2 (425 g)
• 2 (14 ounce) cans beef broth	2 (395 g)
• 2 (15 ounce) cans new potatoes	2 (425 g)
• 1 (16 ounce) package baby carrots	455 g
• 1 tablespoon beef seasoning or seasoned salt	15 ml
• Corn muffins	

Place meatballs, stewed tomatoes, beef broth, potatoes, carrots and beef seasoning in sprayed 6-quart (6 L) slow cooker.

Cover and cook on LOW for 6 to 7 hours. Serve with corn muffins. Serves 6 to 8.

South-of-the-Border Beef Stew

• 1½ - 2 pounds boneless, beef chuck roast	680 - 910 g
• 1 green bell pepper	
• 2 onions, coarsely chopped	
• 2 (15 ounce) cans pinto beans with liquid	2 (425 g)
• ½ cup rice	95 g
• 1 (14 ounce) can beef broth	395 g
• 2 (15 ounce) cans Mexican stewed tomatoes	2 (425 g)
• 1 cup mild or medium green salsa	265 g
• 2 teaspoons ground cumin	10 ml
• Flour tortillas	

Trim fat from beef and cut into 1-inch (2.5 cm) cubes. Brown beef in large skillet and place in sprayed, large slow cooker.

Cut bell pepper into ½-inch (1.2 cm) slices. Add with remaining ingredients plus 1½ cups (375 ml) water and a little salt.

Cover and cook on LOW for 7 to 8 hours. Serve with warm flour tortillas. Serves 6 to 8.

Comfort Stew

- **1½ pounds select stew meat**   **680 g**
- **2 (10 ounce) cans French onion soup**   **2 (280 g)**
- **1 (10 ounce) can cream of onion soup**   **280 g**
- **1 (10 ounce) can cream of celery soup**   **280 g**
- **1 (16 ounce) package frozen stew vegetables, thawed**   **455 g**

Place stew meat in skillet with a little hot oil and brown on all sides. Place in sprayed slow cooker.

Add soups as listed and spread evenly over meat. DO NOT STIR. Turn slow cooker to LOW, cover and cook for 6 to 7 hours.

Add vegetables and continue cooking for additional 1 hour. Serves 4 to 6.

Vegetarian Chili

- **2 (15 ounce) cans stewed tomatoes**   **2 (425 g)**
- **1 (15 ounce) can kidney beans, rinsed, drained**   **425 g**
- **1 (15 ounce) can pinto beans with liquid**   **425 g**
- **1 onion, chopped**
- **1 green bell pepper, seeded, chopped**
- **1 tablespoon chili powder**   **15 ml**
- **1 (7 ounce) package elbow macaroni**   **200 g**
- **¼ cup (½ stick) butter, melted**   **60 g**
- **Shredded cheddar cheese**

Combine tomatoes, kidney beans, pinto beans, onion, bell pepper, chili powder and 1 cup (250 ml) water in sprayed 4 to 5-quart (4 to 5 L) slow cooker.

Cover and cook on LOW for 4 to 5 hours or on HIGH for 2 hours.

Cook macaroni according to package directions, drain and stir in melted butter. Fold macaroni into chili.

If desired, top each serving with shredded cheddar cheese. Serves 4 to 6.

2-Bean Vegetarian Chili

- 2 (15 ounce) cans navy beans with liquid   2 (425 g)
- 1 (15 ounce) can pinto beans with liquid   425 g
- 2 (15 ounce) cans Mexican stewed tomatoes   2 (425 g)
- 1 (15 ounce) can whole kernel corn   425 g
- 1 onion, chopped
- 3 ribs celery, sliced
- 1 tablespoon chili powder   15 ml
- 2 teaspoons dried oregano leaves   10 ml
- 1 teaspoon seasoned salt   5 ml
- Broccoli cornbread

Combine beans, tomatoes, corn, onion, celery, chili powder, oregano, seasoned salt and 1½ cups (375 ml) water in sprayed 5 to 6-quart (5 to 6 L) slow cooker.

Cover and cook on LOW for 4 to 6 hours.

Serve with hot, buttered broccoli cornbread. Serves 6 to 8.

Chili with Chilies

- 2 pounds lean beef chili meat   910 g
- 1 large onion, finely chopped
- 1 (10 ounce) can diced tomatoes and green chilies   280 g
- 2½ cups tomato juice   625 ml
- 2 tablespoons chili powder   15 g
- 1 tablespoon ground cumin   15 ml
- 1 tablespoon minced garlic   15 ml

Brown meat in a little hot oil in skillet. Drain and pour into sprayed slow cooker. Add remaining ingredients and mix well.

Cover and cook on LOW for 7 to 9 hours. Serves 4 to 6.

5-Minute/6-Hour Chili

- **4 pounds lean ground beef**   **1.8 kg**
- **2 (10 ounce) packages seasoned chili mix**   **2 (280 g)**
- **1 (6 ounce) can tomato sauce**   **170 g**
- **2 (15 ounce) cans stewed tomatoes with liquid**   **425 g**
- **2½ teaspoons ground cumin**   **12 ml**

Break ground beef into pieces and brown in large skillet and drain. Use slotted spoon to drain fat and place beef in sprayed 5 to 6-quart (5 to 6 L) slow cooker.

Add chili mix, tomato sauce, stewed tomatoes, cumin, 1 teaspoon (5 ml) salt and 1 cup (250 ml) water.

Cover and cook on LOW for 4 to 5 hours. Serves 6 to 8.

TIP: If you think you can't eat chili without beans, add 2 (15 ounce/425 g) cans ranch-style beans.

Stew Meat Chili

- **2 pounds premium cut stew meat**   **910 g**
- **1 onion, chopped**
- **2 (15 ounce) cans diced tomatoes**   **2 (425 g)**
- **2 (15 ounce) cans pinto beans with liquid**   **2 (425 g)**
- **1½ tablespoons chili powder**   **22 ml**
- **2 teaspoons ground cumin**   **10 ml**
- **1 teaspoon ground oregano**   **5 ml**
- **Shredded cheddar cheese**

If stew meat is in fairly large chunks, cut each chunk in half. Brown stew meat in large skillet and transfer to sprayed, large slow cooker.

Add onion, tomatoes, beans, chili powder, cumin, oregano and a little salt. Cover and cook on LOW for 6 to 7 hours.

Sprinkle shredded cheddar cheese over each serving. Serves 4 to 6.

Chili Frijoles

- 2 cups dry pinto beans   525 g
- 2 onions, finely chopped
- 2 tablespoons chili powder   30 ml
- 1 teaspoon minced garlic   5 ml
- 1 (15 ounce) can tomato sauce   425 g
- 1½ pounds lean ground beef   680 g

Soak beans overnight in water. Drain and transfer beans to sprayed, large slow cooker. Add onion, chili powder, garlic, tomato sauce and 8 cups (1.9 L) water.

Brown ground beef in skillet, drain and transfer to cooker. Cover and cook on LOW for 8 to 9 hours or until beans are tender and stir occasionally.

Stir in 1 teaspoon (5 ml) salt just before serving. Serves 6 to 8.

TIP: *If you forget to soak beans overnight, here's Plan B. Place beans in large saucepan and cover with water. Bring to a boil, turn off heat and let stand for 1 hour.*

Spit-Pea and Ham Chowder

- 1 medium potato
- 3 cups cooked, cubed ham   420 g
- 1 (16 ounce) bag split peas, rinsed   455 g
- 1 (11 ounce) can whole kernel corn with red and green peppers   310 g
- 1 (14 ounce) can chicken broth   395 g
- 2 carrots, sliced
- 2 ribs celery, diagonally sliced
- 1 tablespoon dried onion flakes   15 ml
- 1 teaspoon dried marjoram leaves   5 ml
- 1 teaspoon seasoned salt   5 ml

Cut potato into small cubes and add to sprayed slow cooker.

Add remaining ingredients plus 3 cups (750 ml) water and 1 teaspoon (5 ml) salt.

Cover and cook on LOW for 6 to 8 hours. Serves 4 to 6.

Ham-Vegetable Chowder

A great recipe for leftover ham.

- 1 medium potato
- 1 cup diced ham   140 g
- 2 (10 ounce) cans cream of celery soup   2 (280 g)
- 1 (14 ounce) can chicken broth   395 g
- 3 cups finely diced ham   420 g
- 1 (15 ounce) can whole kernel corn   425 g
- 2 carrots, peeled, sliced
- 1 onion, coarsely chopped
- 1 teaspoon dried basil   5 ml
- 1 teaspoon seasoned salt   5 ml
- 1 (10 ounce) package frozen broccoli florets   280 g

Cut potato into 1-inch (2.5 cm) pieces.

Combine 1 teaspoon (5 ml) pepper and all ingredients except broccoli florets in sprayed, large slow cooker.

Cover and cook on LOW for 5 to 6 hours. Add broccoli to cooker and cook for additional 1 hour. Serves 4 to 6.

TIP: If you don't like black specks in your chowder, use white pepper instead of black pepper.

Oyster-Potato Chowder

- 1 small red bell pepper, seeded, chopped
- 1 onion, chopped
- 1 (14 ounce) can chicken broth   395 g
- 1 medium potato, cubed
- 8 ounces shucked oysters with liquid   225 g
- 1 (10 ounce) package frozen whole kernel corn, thawed   280 g
- 1 teaspoon dried oregano   5 ml
- ½ cup whipping cream   125 ml

Combine all ingredients except cream in sprayed slow cooker.

Cover and cook on LOW for 3 to 4 hours. When ready to serve, stir in cream and cook until warm. Serves 4.

Creamy Crab Chowder

- 2 small zucchini, thinly sliced
- 1 red bell pepper, julienned
- 2 ribs celery, diagonally sliced
- 1 medium potato, cubed
- 2 tablespoons butter, melted   30 g
- 1 (10 ounce) can chicken broth   280 g
- 1 teaspoon seasoned salt   5 ml
- 2 tablespoons cornstarch   15 g
- 3 cups milk   750 ml
- 2 (6 ounce) cans crabmeat, drained   2 (170 g)
- 1 (3 ounce) package cream cheese, cubed   85 g

Place zucchini, bell pepper, celery, potato, butter, broth and seasoned salt in sprayed slow cooker. Stir cornstarch into milk in bowl; pour into slow cooker.

Cover and cook on LOW for 3 to 4 hours.

Turn heat to HIGH, add crabmeat and cream cheese and stir until cream cheese melts. Serves 4.

Country Chicken Chowder

- **1½ pounds boneless, skinless chicken breast halves**   **680 g**
- **2 tablespoons butter**   **30 g**
- **2 (10 ounce) cans cream of potato soup**   **2 (280 g)**
- **1 (14 ounce) can chicken broth**   **395 g**
- **1 (10 ounce) package frozen whole kernel corn**   **280 g**
- **1 onion, sliced**
- **2 ribs celery, sliced**
- **1 (10 ounce) package frozen peas and carrots, thawed**   **280 g**
- **½ teaspoon dried thyme leaves**   **2 ml**
- **½ cup half-and-half cream**   **125 ml**

Cut chicken into 1-inch (2.5 cm) strips. Brown chicken strips in butter in skillet and transfer to sprayed, large slow cooker.

Add soup, broth, corn, onion, celery, peas and carrots, and thyme and stir. Cover and cook on LOW for 3 to 4 hours or until vegetables are tender.

Turn off heat, stir in half-and-half cream and set aside for about 10 minutes before serving. Serves 4 to 6.

Corn-Ham Chowder

- **1 (14 ounce) can chicken broth**   **395 g**
- **1 cup milk**   **250 ml**
- **1 (10 ounce) can cream of celery soup**   **280 g**
- **1 (15 ounce) can cream-style corn**   **425 g**
- **1 (15 ounce) can whole kernel corn**   **425 g**
- **½ cup dry potato flakes**   **30 g**
- **1 onion, chopped**
- **2 - 3 cups cooked, chopped ham**   **280 - 420 g**

Combine broth, milk, soup, cream-style corn, whole kernel corn, potato flakes, onion and ham in sprayed 6-quart (6 L) slow cooker.

Cover and cook on LOW for 4 to 5 hours. When ready to serve, season with a little salt and pepper. Serves 4 to 6.

Chicken-Corn Chowder

- **3 cups cooked, cubed chicken**   420 g
- **1 (14 ounce) can chicken broth**   395 g
- **2 (10 ounce) cans cream of potato soup**   2 (280 g)
- **1 large onion, chopped**
- **3 ribs celery, sliced diagonally**
- **1 (16 ounce) package frozen whole kernel corn, thawed**   455 g
- **⅔ cup whipping cream**   150 ml

Combine chicken, broth, potato soup, onion, celery, corn and ¾ cup (175 ml) water in sprayed 5 to 6-quart (5 to 6 L) slow cooker.

Cover and cook on LOW for 3 to 4 hours.

Add whipping cream to slow cooker and heat for additional 15 minutes or until thoroughly hot. Serves 4 to 6.

Shrimp and Ham Jambalaya

- **3 ribs celery, diagonally slice**
- **1 onion, chopped**
- **1 red bell pepper, seeded, chopped**
- **1 green bell pepper, seeded, chopped**
- **2 (15 ounce) cans stewed tomatoes**   **2 (425 g)**
- **2 cups cooked, cubed smoked ham**   **280 g**
- **½ teaspoon cayenne pepper**   **2 ml**
- **1 tablespoon dried parsley flakes**   **15 ml**
- **2 teaspoons minced garlic**   **30 ml**
- **1 pound peeled, veined shrimp**   **455 g**
- **Rice, cooked**

Combine celery, onion, bell peppers, tomatoes, ham, cayenne pepper, parsley flakes, garlic and a little salt and pepper in sprayed slow cooker.

Cover and cook on LOW for 7 to 8 hours or on HIGH for 3 to 4 hours.

Stir in shrimp and cook on LOW for 1 hour. Serve over rice. Serves 4 to 6.

Shrimp and Sausage Jambalaya

- **1 pound cooked, smoked sausage links**   **455 g**
- **1 onion, chopped**
- **1 green bell pepper, chopped**
- **2 teaspoons minced garlic**   **10 ml**
- **1 (28 ounce) can diced tomatoes**   **795 g**
- **1 tablespoon parsley flakes**   **15 ml**
- **½ teaspoon dried thyme leaves**   **2 ml**
- **1 teaspoon Cajun seasoning**   **5 ml**
- **¼ teaspoon cayenne pepper**   **1 ml**
- **1 pound peeled, veined shrimp**   **455 g**
- **Rice, cooked**

Combine all ingredients except shrimp and rice in sprayed slow cooker.

Cover and cook on LOW for 6 to 8 hours or on HIGH for 3 to 4 hours.

Stir in shrimp and cook on LOW for additional 1 hour. Serve over rice.
Serves 4 to 6.

Jambalaya Ready

- **2 - 3 pounds boneless, skinless chicken thighs**   **910 g - 1.4 kg**
- **1 (28 ounce) can crushed tomatoes**   **795 g**
- **2 onions, diced**
- **2 bell peppers, seeded, diced**
- **4 ribs celery, chopped**
- **3 cloves garlic, minced**
- **2 cups cooked white rice**   **315 g**
- **1 pound raw shrimp, peeled**   **455 g**
- **¼ - ½ teaspoon cayenne**   **1 - 2 ml**

Placer chicken, tomatoes, onions, bell peppers, celery and garlic in slow cooker. Cover and cook on LOW for 4 to 6 hours.

Add cooked rice, shrimp, cayenne and a little salt and pepper. Continue to cook covered for about 15 minutes or until shrimp turn pink. Serves 8.

TIP: Add chicken broth or water if you want this thinner.

Gumbo Ready

- **1 pound okra, sliced** — 455 g
- **½ cup (1 stick) plus 1 tablespoon butter, divided** — 115 g/15 ml
- **2 onions, chopped**
- **4 ribs celery, sliced**
- **2 - 3 cloves garlic, minced**
- **2 tablespoons fresh snipped parsley**
- **¼ cup flour** — 30 g
- **1 (28 ounce) can crushed tomatoes** — 795 g
- **1 pound raw shrimp, peeled** — 455 g
- **1 pound fresh crabmeat, flaked** — 455 g

Brown okra in ¼ cup butter over medium heat in large skillet. Pour into slow cooker. Saute onions, celery, garlic and parsley in 1 tablespoon butter until onions are translucent. Pour into slow cooker.

Melt ¼ cup butter in skillet and sprinkle flour over butter. Turn heat to low and stir constantly until flour turns brown and all lumps are gone. Pour into slow cooker.

Pour tomatoes into slow cooker and cover. Cook on LOW for 4 to 5 hours or until okra is just tender.

Add shrimp and crabmeat, cover and cook about 15 minutes or until shrimp turn pink. Serve over cooked rice. Serves 8 to 10.

Vegetables & Side Dishes

Broccoli-Cheese Bake

- ¼ cup (½ stick) butter, melted   55 g
- 1 (10 ounce) can cream of mushroom soup   280 g
- 1 (10 ounce) can cream of onion soup   280 g
- 1 cup instant rice   95 g
- 1 (8 ounce) package cubed Velveeta® cheese   225 g
- 2 (10 ounce) packages frozen chopped broccoli, thawed   2 (280 g)

Combine all ingredients, plus ½ cup (125 ml) water in sprayed slow cooker and stir well.

Cover and cook on HIGH for 2 to 3 hours. Serves 4 to 6.

Savory Broccoli and Cauliflower

- 1 (16 ounce) package frozen broccoli florets, thawed   455 g
- 1 (16 ounce) package frozen cauliflower florets, thawed   455 g
- 2 (10 ounce) cans nacho cheese soup   2 (280 g)
- 6 slices bacon, cooked, crumbled

Place broccoli and cauliflower in sprayed slow cooker. Sprinkle with a little salt and pepper.

Spoon soup over top and sprinkle with bacon. Cover and cook on LOW for 3 to 4 hours. Serves 6 to 8.

Creamy Broccoli and New Potatoes

- **2 (16 ounce) packages frozen broccoli florets, thawed**   **2 (425 g)**
- **2 (15 ounce) cans whole new potatoes, drained**   **2 (425 g)**
- **2 (10 ounce) cans cream of celery soup**   **2 (280 g)**
- **1 rib celery, chopped**
- **½ cup milk**   **125 ml**
- **1 (8 ounce) package shredded cheddar cheese, divided**   **225 g**
- **1½ cups cracker crumbs, divided**   **90 g**

Place broccoli on plate, cut off stems and discard. Combine broccoli and potatoes in sprayed slow cooker.

Combine soup and milk in saucepan, heat just enough to mix well and pour over broccoli and potatoes.

Sprinkle half cheese and crumbs over broccoli. Cover and cook on LOW for 3 to 4 hours.

When ready to serve, sprinkle remaining cheese and crumbs over top. Serves 6 to 8.

Easy Broccoli-Rice Casserole

- **2 - 3 heads broccoli, stemmed**
- **1 - 1½ cups cooked rice**   **160 - 235 g**
- **1 (10 ounce) can cream of celery soup**   **280 g**
- **1 (8 ounce) jar cheese sauce**   **225 g**

Cut broccoli florets in half, place in sprayed slow cooker and mix in rice. In saucepan heat soup, ½ soup can water and cheese sauce over medium heat until ingredients mix well. Pour over broccoli. Cover and cook on LOW for 3 to 4 hours or until broccoli is tender. Serves 4 to 6.

TIP: If you want something crunchy in the casserole, add almond slivers or chopped celery.

Company Broccoli

- **1½ pounds fresh broccoli, trimmed well**   **680 g**
- **1 (10 ounce) can cream of chicken soup**   **280 g**
- **½ cup mayonnaise**   **110 g**
- **1 (8 ounce) package shredded cheddar cheese, divided**   **225 g**
- **¼ cup toasted slivered almonds**   **40 g**

Place broccoli in sprayed slow cooker. Combine chicken soup, mayonnaise, half cheese and ¼ cup (60 ml) water in bowl. Spoon over broccoli.

Cover and cook on LOW for 2 to 3 hours. When ready to serve, sprinkle remaining cheese over broccoli and top with toasted almonds. Serves 6 to 8.

Easy Cabbage Bake

- 2 medium heads cabbage, stemmed, quartered
- 1 (8 ounce) jar Cheez Whiz®   225 g
- 1 tablespoon butter   15 ml
- 2 slices bacon, fried, crumbled

Place cabbage in sprayed slow cooker, pour Cheez Whiz® over top and butter over that. Cover and cook on LOW for 4 to 5 hours or until cabbage is tender.

Stir about half way through cooking. Season with pepper and crumbled bacon on top before serving. Serves 6 to 8.

Sunshine Green Beans

- 2 (16 ounce) packages frozen whole green beans, thawed   2 (455 g)
- 2 (10 ounce) cans fiesta nacho cheese soup   2 (280 g)
- 1 (10 ounce) package frozen seasoning blend (chopped onions
  and bell peppers)   280 g
- 1 (8 ounce) can sliced water chestnuts, cut in half   225 g
- 1 teaspoon seasoned salt   5 ml

Combine all ingredients plus ¼ cup (60 ml) water in sprayed, large slow cooker and stir to mix well. Cover and cook on LOW for 4 to 5 hours. Serves 6 to 8.

Crunchy Green Beans

- 2 (16 ounce) packages frozen whole green beans, thawed — 2 (455 g)
- 3 ribs celery, diagonally sliced
- 1 red bell pepper, julienned
- 2 (11 ounce) cans sliced water chestnuts, drained — 2 (310 g)
- 1 (10 ounce) can cream of chicken soup — 280 g
- ½ cup slivered almonds — 85 g
- 1 (3 ounce) can french-fried onions — 85 g

Combine green beans, celery, bell pepper, water chestnuts, chicken soup and almonds in sprayed slow cooker.

Cover and cook on LOW for 2 to 4 hours. About 10 minutes before serving, top with fried onions. Serves 6 to 8.

Southern Green Beans and Potatoes

- 6 - 8 medium new potatoes with peels, sliced
- 5 cups fresh whole green beans, trimmed — 355 g
- 2 tablespoons dry, minced onions — 30 ml
- ¼ cup (½ stick) butter, melted — 60 g
- 1 (10 ounce) can cream of celery soup — 280 g
- 1 (10 ounce) can fiesta nacho cheese soup — 280 g

Place potatoes, green beans and minced onions in sprayed slow cooker.

Pour melted butter over vegetables.

Combine soups and ⅓ cup (75 ml) water in saucepan. Heat just enough to be able to mix soups and pour over vegetables.

Cover and cook on LOW for 7 to 8 hours. Serves 6 to 8.

> *You can thicken liquid in the slow cooker by mixing 1 tablespoon (15 ml) cornstarch thoroughly with 2 tablespoons (30 ml) cold water. Add to liquid and cook until liquid reaches gravy or sauce consistency.*

Bacon-Seasoned Green Beans

- **2 pounds fresh green beans**   **910 g**
- **1 onion, finely chopped**
- **4 thick slices bacon**
- **5 - 6 medium new (red) potatoes**
- **1 teaspoon sugar**   **5 ml**

Snap and wash green beans, place beans and onion in sprayed 5 to 6-quart (5 to 6 L) slow cooker.

Cut bacon in 1-inch (2.5 cm) pieces and fry in skillet until crisp. Remove some of deeper "eyes" in new potatoes and cut into quarters.

Add cooked bacon pieces, potatoes and 1 cup (250 ml) water to slow cooker. Add about 1 teaspoon (5 ml) salt and sugar. (A touch of sugar always helps fresh vegetables.)

Cover and cook on LOW for 3 to 4 hours. Serves 6 to 8.

Hot Cheese Green Beans

- **2 (16 ounce) packages frozen whole green beans, thawed**   **2 (425 g)**
- **2 (8 ounce) cans sliced water chestnuts, drained**   **2 (225 g)**
- **1 (16 ounce) package cubed jalapeno Velveeta® cheese**   **455 g**
- **1 (10 ounce) can tomatoes and green chilies**   **280 g**
- **1 onion, chopped**
- **¼ cup (½ stick) butter, melted**   **55 g**
- **1 tablespoon chicken seasoning**   **15 ml**
- **1½ cups slightly crushed potato chips**   **85 g**

Combine green beans, water chestnuts, cheese, tomatoes and green chilies, onion, melted butter and seasoning in sprayed slow cooker and mix well.

Cover and cook on LOW for 3 to 5 hours. Just before serving, cover top with crushed potato chips. Serves 6 to 8.

TIP: If you would like this to be a one-dish meal, add 2 to 3 cups (280 to 420 g) cooked, cubed ham.

Sweet-Hot Bean Combo

- **3 (15 ounce) cans black beans, rinsed, drained**   3 (425 g)
- **3 (15 ounce) cans great northern beans, rinsed, drained**   3 (425 g)
- **1 (16 ounce) jar hot, thick-and-chunky salsa**   455 g
- **½ cup packed brown sugar**   110 g

Combine black beans, northern beans, salsa and brown sugar in sprayed 5 to 6-quart (5 to 6 L) slow cooker.

Cover and cook on LOW for 3 to 4 hours. Serves 6 to 8.

TIP: To include pinto beans in this dish, use only 2 (15 ounce) cans black beans and 1 (15 ounce) can pinto beans.

Bean Pot Medley

- **4 thick slices bacon, cooked crisp, crumbled**
- **1 onion, chopped, cooked with bacon**
- **1 (15 ounce) can kidney beans, drained**   425 g
- **1 (15 ounce) can lima beans with liquid**   425 g
- **1 (15 ounce) can pinto beans with liquid**   425 g
- **1 (15 ounce) can navy beans with liquid**   425 g
- **1 (15 ounce) can pork and beans with liquid**   425 g
- **1 onion, chopped**
- **¾ cup chili sauce**   205 g
- **1 cup packed brown sugar**   220 g
- **1 tablespoon Worcestershire sauce**   15 ml

Combine all ingredients in sprayed slow cooker and mix well. Cover and cook on LOW for 5 to 6 hours. Serves 6 to 8.

---

*Keep the lid on the slow cooker (unless recipes calls for stirring).
The slow cooker can take as long as 20 minutes to regain the heat lost
when the cover is removed. Do not cook without cover in place.*

Better Butter Beans

- 2 cups sliced celery — 200 g
- 2 onions, chopped
- 1 green bell pepper, julienned
- 1 (15 ounce) can stewed tomatoes — 425 g
- ¼ cup (½ stick) butter, melted — 60 g
- 1 tablespoon chicken seasoning — 15 ml
- 3 (15 ounce) cans butter beans, drained — 3 (425 g)

Combine all ingredients in sprayed slow cooker and mix well.

Cover and cook on LOW for 3 to 4 hours. Serves 6 to 8.

TIP: You can make this a one-dish dinner, add 2 to 3 cups (280 to 420 g) cooked, cubed ham.

Garbanzo-Cannellini Bean Mix

- 2 (15 ounce) cans garbanzo beans, drained — 2 (425 g)
- 1 (15 ounce) can red kidney beans, drained — 425 g
- 1 (15 ounce) can cannellini beans, drained — 425 g
- 2 (15 ounce) cans great northern beans, drained — 2 (425 g)
- 1 teaspoon Italian seasoning — 5 ml
- 1 (1 ounce) packet onion soup mix — 30 g
- 1 onion, chopped
- 1 teaspoon minced garlic — 5 ml
- ½ cup beef broth — 125 ml

Combine all ingredients in sprayed slow cooker and stir well. Cover and cook on LOW for 5 to 6 hours or on HIGH for 2 hours 30 minutes to 3 hours. Serves 6 to 8.

Most slow cooker users suggest "tasting" before serving in order to add any needed seasonings such as salt, pepper, lemon juice, herb blends, Worcestershire sauce, etc.

Creamy Limas

- **2 (16 ounce) packages frozen baby lima beans, thawed**   2 (455 g)
- **1 (10 ounce) can cream of celery**   280 g
- **1 (10 ounce) can cream of onion soup**   280 g
- **1 red bell pepper, cored, seeded, julienned**
- **1 (4 ounce) jar sliced mushrooms, drained**   115 g
- **¼ cup milk**   60 ml
- **1 cup shredded cheddar-colby cheese**   115 g

Combine lima beans, soups, bell pepper, mushrooms and ½ teaspoon (2 ml) salt in saucepan and heat just enough to mix well. Pour into sprayed 4 to 5-quart (4 to 5 L) slow cooker. Stir well.

Cover and cook on LOW for 8 to 9 hours.

Just before serving, stir in milk. Spoon limas to serving bowl and sprinkle cheese over top. Serves 6 to 8.

Recipes in this cookbook may be cooked in 3 to 6-quart slow cookers. You may need to adjust the quantity of ingredients for a smaller cooker.

Bell Peppers Stuffed with Black Beans

- **5 small bell peppers**
- **1 onion, chopped**
- **3 ribs celery, diced**
- **½ teaspoon chili powder**   **2 ml**
- **2 (15 ounce) cans black beans, rinsed, drained**   **2 (425 g)**
- **1½ cups shredded cheddar cheese, divided**   **170 g**
- **1 cup chunky salsa**   **265 g**
- **½ cup sour cream**   **120 g**

Cut stem off bell peppers and leave whole. Remove core and seeds and pat dry inside and out. Dice 1 bell pepper.

Saute onion, celery and diced bell pepper with chili powder until onion is translucent. Remove from heat and pour 1 can black beans into skillet.

Mash beans with fork and mix with onions. Cool about 10 minutes and mix with 1 cup (115 g) cheese. Spoon mixture into cavities of bell peppers and place in sprayed slow cooker.

Sprinkle salsa over top and cook on LOW for about 4 to 6 hours or until bell peppers are tender. Sprinkle remaining cheese on top and serve with a dollop of sour cream. Serves 4.

Mexican Three Step

- 2 (15 ounce) cans black beans, rinsed, drained   2 (425 g)
- 1 (28 ounce) can crushed tomatoes with liquid   795 g
- 1 (15 ounce) can whole kernel corn, drained   425 g
- 1 (6 ounce) can tomato paste   170 g
- 2 cloves garlic, minced
- 1 teaspoon cumin   5 ml
- 1 jalapeno pepper, seeded, chopped
- 3 corn tortillas

Mix beans, tomatoes, corn, tomato paste, garlic, cumin and jalapeno in large bowl.

Pour one-third of mixture into slow cooker and top with tortilla. Repeat steps two more times. Cover and cook on LOW for 5 to 6 hours. Serves 4 to 6.

Cajun Beans and Rice

- 1 pound dry black or kidney beans   455 g
- 2 onions, chopped
- 2 teaspoons minced garlic   10 ml
- 1 tablespoon ground cumin   15 ml
- 1 (14 ounce) can chicken broth   400 g
- 1 cup instant brown rice   95 g

Place beans in saucepan, cover with water and soak overnight.

Combine beans, onion, garlic, cumin, chicken broth, 2 teaspoons (10 ml) salt and 2 cups (500 ml) water in sprayed 4 to 5-quart (4 to 5 L) slow cooker.

Cover and cook on LOW for 4 to 6 hours.

Stir in instant rice, cover and cook for additional 20 minutes. Serves 4 to 6.

TIP: If soaking beans overnight is not an option, place beans in saucepan and add enough water to cover by 2 inches (5 cm). Bring to a boil, reduce heat and simmer for 10 minutes. Let stand for 1 hour, drain and rinse beans.

Cinnamon Carrots

- **2 (16 ounce) packages baby carrots**
- **¾ cup packed brown sugar**
- **¼ cup honey**
- **½ cup orange juice**
- **2 tablespoons butter, melted**
- **¾ teaspoon ground cinnamon**

2 (455 g)
165 g
85 g
125 ml
30 g
4 ml

Place carrots in sprayed 3 to 4-quart (3 to 4 L) slow cooker.

Combine brown sugar, honey, orange juice, butter and cinnamon in bowl and mix well. Pour over carrots and mix so sugar-cinnamon mixture coats carrots.

Cover and cook on LOW for 3 hours 30 minutes to 4 hours and stir twice during cooking time.

About 20 minutes before serving, transfer carrots with slotted spoon to serving dish and cover to keep warm.

Pour liquid from cooker into saucepan; boil for several minutes until liquid reduces by half. Spoon over carrots in serving dish. Serves 6 to 8.

Cooking time on HIGH equals about half the cooking time on LOW.

Krazy Karrots

- 1 (16 ounce) package baby carrots   455 g
- ¼ cup (½ stick) butter, melted   60 g
- ⅔ cup packed brown sugar   150 g
- 1 (1 ounce) packet ranch dressing mix   30 g

Combine carrots, melted butter, brown sugar, ranch dressing mix and ¼ cup (60 ml) water in sprayed 4-quart (4 L) slow cooker and stir well.

Cover and cook on LOW for 3 to 4 hours and stir occasionally. Serves 4.

Brown-Sugared Carrots

- 1 (32 ounce) package baby carrots   910 g
- ½ cup packed brown sugar   110 g
- ¼ cup (½ stick) butter, softened   55 g
- 1 teaspoon cinnamon   5 ml
- 1 tablespoon minced parsley   15 ml

Place carrots in sprayed slow cooker. Melt butter in saucepan and add brown sugar. Stir to mix and remove from heat. Add cinnamon and parsley and pour over carrots.

Cover and cook on LOW for 4 to 5 hours or until carrots are tender. Stir occasionally to mix sauce with carrots. Serves 6 to 8.

104

Yellow Squash-Zucchini Combo

- 1½ pounds small yellow squash   **680 g**
- 1½ pounds zucchini   **680 g**
- 1 teaspoon seasoned salt   **5 ml**
- ¼ cup (½ stick) butter, melted   **60 g**
- ½ cup seasoned breadcrumbs   **60 g**
- ½ cup shredded cheddar cheese   **60 g**

Cut both yellow squash and zucchini in small pieces. Place in sprayed slow cooker and sprinkle with seasoned salt and pepper.

Pour melted butter over squash and sprinkle with breadcrumbs and cheese. Cover and cook on LOW for 5 to 6 hours. Serves 6 to 8.

Sunny Yellow Squash

- 2 pounds medium yellow squash, sliced   **910 g**
- 2 onions, coarsely chopped
- 3 ribs celery, diagonally sliced
- 1 green bell pepper, cored, seeded, julienned
- 1 (8 ounce) package cream cheese, cubed   **225 g**
- 1 teaspoon sugar   **5 ml**
- ¼ cup (½ stick) butter, melted   **60 g**
- 1 (10 ounce) can cheddar cheese soup   **280 g**
- 1½ cups crushed croutons   **45 g**

Combine all ingredients, except breadcrumbs in sprayed slow cooker and mix well. Add 1 teaspoon (5 ml) each of salt and pepper.

Cover and cook on LOW for 3 to 4 hours. Before serving, sprinkle top with croutons. Serves 6 to 8.

TIP: If you don't like black specks, use white pepper instead of black pepper.

Golden Stuffed Squash

- 1 pound yellow squash, thinly sliced   455 g
- 1 pound zucchini, thinly sliced   455 g
- 3 ribs celery, sliced
- 1 onion, chopped
- 1 (10 ounce) can cream of chicken soup   280 g
- 1 (8 ounce) carton sour cream   225 g
- 3 tablespoons flour   20 g
- 1 (6 ounce) package seasoned stuffing mix   170 g
- ½ cup (1 stick) butter, melted   115 g

Combine squash, zucchini, celery, onion and soup in large bowl. In separate bowl, mix sour cream with flour and stir into vegetables.

Toss stuffing with melted butter in bowl and spoon half into sprayed slow cooker.

Top with vegetables and spoon remaining stuffing on top. Cover and cook on LOW for 5 to 7 hours. Serves 6 to 8.

Baked Eggplant

- 1½ pounds eggplant, peeled, cubed   680 g
- 2 onions, sliced
- 3 ribs celery, sliced
- 1 (15 ounce) can stewed diced tomatoes   425 g
- ¼ cup tomato sauce   115 g
- 2 tablespoons balsamic vinegar   30 ml
- 1 tablespoon olive oil   15 ml
- 1 tablespoon sugar   15 ml
- 1 tablespoon capers   15 ml
- 1 cup shredded parmesan cheese   100 g

Place eggplant, onion, celery and tomatoes in slow cooker. In separate bowl, mix tomato sauce, vinegar, olive, sugar and capers. Pour over eggplant mixture. Cook on LOW for 4 hours or until eggplant is tender. Season with a little salt and pepper.

Sprinkle half of parmesan cheese over eggplant about 10 minutes before serving to melt. Sprinkle remaining parmesan just before serving. Serves 4 to 6.

Super Corn

- 2 (15 ounce) cans whole kernel corn   2 (425 g)
- 2 (15 ounce) cans creamed corn   2 (425 g)
- ½ cup (1 stick) butter, melted   115 g
- 1 (8 ounce) carton sour cream   225 g
- 1 (8 ounce) package jalapeno cornbread mix 225 g

Combine all ingredients in large bowl and mix well.

Pour into sprayed slow cooker, cover and cook on LOW for 4 to 5 hours. Serves 6 to 8.

TIP: *Make this a one-dish meal by adding 2 to 3 cups (280 to 420 g) leftover, cubed ham.*

Kids' Favorite Corn

- **1 (8 ounce) and 1 (3 ounce) package cream cheese** — 225 g/85 g
- **½ cup (1 stick) butter, melted** — 115 g
- **2 (16 ounce) packages frozen whole kernel corn, thawed** — 2 (455 g)

Turn sprayed 4-quart (4 L) slow cooker to HIGH and add cream cheese and butter. Cook just until cheese and butter melt; stir.

Add corn and a little salt and pepper. Cover and cook on LOW for 1 hour 30 minutes to 2 hours. Serves 4 to 6.

Creamed Peas and New Potatoes

- **2 pounds small new (red) potatoes with peels, quartered** — 910 g
- **1 (16 ounce) package frozen green peas with pearl onions, thawed** — 455 g
- **1 onion, chopped**
- **2 ribs celery, chopped**
- **2 (10 ounce) cans fiesta nacho cheese soup** — 2 (280 g)
- **½ cup milk** — 125 ml

Sprinkle potatoes with a little salt and pepper, place in sprayed slow cooker and place peas on top.

Combine nacho cheese soup and milk in saucepan, heat just enough to mix well and spoon over peas. Cover and cook on LOW for 4 to 5 hours. Serves 6 to 8.

Creamy Cheese Spinach

- 2 (10 ounce) packages frozen chopped spinach   2 (280 g)
- 1 (16 ounce) carton small curd cottage cheese   455 g
- 1½ cups shredded American or cheddar cheese   170 g
- 3 eggs, beaten
- ¼ cup (½ stick) butter, melted   60 g
- ¼ cup flour   30 g

Squeeze spinach between paper towels to completely remove excess moisture. Combine all ingredients in bowl and mix well. Spoon into sprayed slow cooker.

Cover and cook on HIGH for 1 hour, change heat to LOW and cook for additional 3 to 5 hours or until knife inserted in center comes out clean. Serves 4 to 6.

Spinach-Cheese Bake

- 1 (10 ounce) and 1 (16 ounce) package chopped spinach, thawed, drained   280 g/455 g
- 1 (8 ounce) package cream cheese, cubed, softened   225 g
- 1 (10 ounce) can cream of chicken soup   280 g
- 1 egg, beaten
- 1 (8 ounce) package shredded cheddar cheese   225 g

Squeeze spinach between paper towels to completely remove excess moisture.

Combine spinach, cream cheese, chicken soup, egg and a little salt and pepper in large bowl. Spoon into sprayed slow cooker.

Cover and cook on LOW for 3 to 4 hours. Before serving, stir in cheddar cheese. Serves 4 to 6.

Slow cooking retains most of the moisture in food, therefore if a recipe results in too much liquid at the end of cooking time, remove cover, increase heat to HIGH and cook another 45 minutes.

Broccoli-Zucchini Surprise

- 1 (16 ounce) package frozen broccoli, cauliflower and carrots   455 g
- 2 medium zucchini, halved lengthwise, sliced
- 1 (1 ounce) packet ranch dressing mix   30 g
- 2 tablespoons butter, melted   30 g

Place broccoli, cauliflower and carrots, and zucchini in sprayed 4-quart (4 L) slow cooker.

Combine ranch dressing mix, melted butter and ½ cup (125 ml) water in bowl, spoon over vegetables and stir.

Cover and cook on LOW for 2 to 3 hours. Serves 4.

Vegetables in Cream Sauce

- 2 (10 ounce) cans cream of mushroom soup   2 (280 g)
- 1 (8 ounce) package cubed Velveeta® cheese   225 g
- 1 cup milk   250 ml
- 2 tablespoons butter, melted   30 g
- 1 teaspoon seasoned salt   15 ml
- ½ cup chopped mushrooms   35 g
- 1 (16 ounce) package frozen vegetable mix, thawed   455 g
- 1 (10 ounce) package frozen green peas, thawed   280 g
- 1 (10 ounce) package frozen whole kernel corn, thawed   280 g
- 1 cup instant white rice   95 g

Combine soup, cheese, milk, butter, seasoned salt and 1 cup (250 ml) water in saucepan; heat just enough to mix.

Place all vegetables in sprayed, large slow cooker. Pour soup mixture on top. Cover and cook on LOW for 4 to 5 hours. Add rice and serve when tender. Serves 6 to 8.

Golden Veggies

• 1 (16 ounce) package frozen cauliflower florets, thawed	455 g
• 1 (15 ounce) can whole kernel corn	425 g
• ¾ pound small yellow squash, chopped	340 g
• ¼ cup (½ stick) butter, melted	60 g
• 2 (10 ounce) cans cheddar cheese soup	2 (280 g)
• 6 slices bacon, cooked, crumbled	

Place cauliflower, corn and squash in sprayed slow cooker and sprinkle with a little salt and pepper.

Pour melted butter over vegetables and spoon cheese soup on top. Sprinkle with crumbled bacon. Cover and cook on LOW for 4 to 5 hours. Serves 4 to 6.

Four Veggie Bake

• 1 (10 ounce) package frozen broccoli florets, thawed	280 g
• 1 (10 ounce) package frozen cauliflower, thawed	280 g
• 1 (10 ounce) package frozen brussels sprouts	280 g
• 4 small yellow squash, sliced	
• 1 (10 ounce) can cream of mushroom soup	280 g
• 1 (16 ounce) package cubed Velveeta® cheese	455 g

Place vegetables in sprayed slow cooker. Layer soup and cheese on top of vegetables.

Cover and cook on LOW for 3 to 4 hours. Serves 4 to 6.

Potatoes al Grande

- 6 medium potatoes, peeled
- 1 (8 ounce) package shredded cheddar cheese, divided   225 g
- 1 (10 ounce) can cream of chicken soup   280 g
- ¼ cup (½ stick) butter, melted   60 g
- 1 (8 ounce) carton sour cream   225 g
- 1 (3 ounce) can french-fried onions   85 g

Cut potatoes in 1-inch (2.5 cm) strips. Toss potatoes with a little salt and pepper plus half cheese. Place in sprayed slow cooker.

Combine soup, melted butter and 2 tablespoons (30 ml) water in saucepan and heat just enough to pour over potato mixture.

Cover and cook on LOW for 6 to 8 hours or until potatoes are tender.

Stir in sour cream and remaining cheese. When ready to serve, sprinkle fried onions over top of potatoes. Serves 4 to 6.

Parsley Potatoes

- 2 pounds new (red) potatoes with peels, quartered   910 g
- ¼ cup canola oil   60 ml
- 1 (.04 ounce) packet ranch dressing mix   10 g
- ¼ cup chopped fresh parsley   15 g

Place potatoes, oil, dressing mix and ¼ cup (60 ml) water in sprayed 4 to 5-quart (4 to 5 L) slow cooker and toss to coat potatoes.

Cover and cook on LOW for 3 to 4 hours or until potatoes are tender. When ready to serve, sprinkle parsley over potatoes and toss. Serves 4 to 6.

Slow cookers meld flavors deliciously, but colors can fade over long cooking times, therefore you can "dress up" your dish with colorful garnishes such as fresh parsley or chives, purchased salsa, extra shredded cheeses, a sprinkle of paprika or a dollop of sour cream.

Roasted New Potatoes

- 18 - 20 new (red) potatoes with peels
- ¼ cup (½ stick) butter, melted   60 g
- 1 tablespoon dried parsley   15 ml
- ½ teaspoon garlic powder   2 ml
- ½ teaspoon paprika   2 ml

Combine all ingredients plus ½ teaspoon (2 ml) each of salt and pepper in sprayed slow cooker and mix well.

Cover and cook on LOW for 7 hours or on HIGH for 3 hours 30 minutes to 4 hours.

When ready to serve, remove potatoes with slotted spoon to serving dish and cover to keep warm.

Add about 2 tablespoons (30 ml) water to drippings and stir until they blend well. Pour mixture over potatoes. Serves 4 to 6.

Onion-Pepper Cheese Potatoes

- 1 (28 ounce) package frozen hash-brown potatoes with onions
  and peppers, thawed   795 g
- 2 (10 ounce) cans cream of chicken soup   2 (280 g)
- 1 onion, chopped
- 1 red bell pepper, cored, seeded, chopped
- 1 (8 ounce) carton sour cream   225 g
- ½ cup (1 stick) butter, melted, divided   115 g
- 1 (8 ounce) package shredded cheddar cheese   225 g
- 2 tablespoons dried parsley   30 ml
- 2 cups dry stuffing mix   120 g

Combine potatoes, soup, sour cream, ¼ cup (57 g) melted butter, cheese, parsley and 1 teaspoon (5 ml) salt in large bowl and mix well.

Spoon mixture into sprayed, large slow cooker. Sprinkle stuffing mix over potato mixture and drizzle remaining butter over stuffing.

Cover and cook on LOW for 7 to 9 hours or on HIGH for 3 to 4 hours. Serves 4 to 6.

Glory Potatoes

- **1 (10 ounce) can cream of chicken soup**   **280 g**
- **1 (8 ounce) carton sour cream**   **225 g**
- **2 pounds potatoes, peeled, cubed**   **910 g**
- **1 (8 ounce) package shredded cheddar Jack cheese**   **225 g**
- **1 cup crushed potato chips**   **55 g**

Combine soup, sour cream, ¼ cup (60 ml) water and a little salt and pepper in bowl.

Combine potatoes and cheese in sprayed 5-quart (5 L) slow cooker. Spoon soup-sour cream mixture over potatoes.

Cover and cook on LOW for 8 to 9 hours. When ready to serve, sprinkle crushed potato chips over potatoes. Serves 4 to 6.

Easy Baked Potatoes

- **6 medium russet potatoes with peels**
- **¼ - ½ cup canola oil**   **60 - 125 ml**
- **Butter**
- **Sour cream**

Pierce potatoes with fork. Brush potato skins with oil and sprinkle a little salt and pepper on potato skins.

Wrap potatoes individually in foil and place in sprayed large slow cooker. Cover and cook on LOW for 7 to 8 hours or until potatoes are tender.

Prepare assorted toppings such as: shredded cheese, salsa, ranch dip, chopped green onions, bacon bits, chopped boiled eggs, cheese-hamburger dip, broccoli-cheese soup, etc. Serves 6.

For easier cleanup, it is best to always spray cooker with a cooking spray or rub inside with a little vegetable oil.

Easy Cheesy Hash-Brown Potatoes

- 5 cups frozen hash-brown potatoes   750 g
- 1 (8 ounce) package shredded cheddar cheese   225 g
- 1 onion, chopped
- 1 bell pepper, seeded, chopped
- 1½ cups milk   375 ml

Mix all ingredients in sprayed slow cooker, cover and cook on LOW for 5 to 6 hours or until dish is firm. Serves 6 to 8.

Creamed New Potatoes

- 2 - 2½ pounds new (red) potatoes with peels, quartered   910 g
- 1 (8 ounce) package cream cheese, softened   225 g
- 1 (10 ounce) can fiesta nacho soup   280 g
- 1 (1 ounce) packet buttermilk ranch salad dressing mix   30 g
- 1 cup milk   250 ml

Place potatoes in sprayed 6-quart (6 L) slow cooker.

Beat cream cheese until creamy and fold in fiesta nacho soup, ranch salad dressing mix and milk. Stir into potatoes.

Cover and cook on LOW for 3 to 4 hours or until potatoes are well done. Serves 4 to 6.

Company Potatoes

- **1 (5 ounce) box scalloped potatoes**   145 g
- **1 (5 ounce) box au gratin potatoes**   145 g
- **1 cup milk**   250 ml
- **6 tablespoons (¾ stick) butter, melted**   85 g
- **½ pound bacon, cooked crisp, crumbled**   225 g

Place both boxes of potatoes in sprayed slow cooker. Combine milk, butter and 4¼ cups (1.1 L) water in bowl and pour over potatoes.

Cover and cook on LOW for 4 to 5 hours. When ready to serve, sprinkle crumbled bacon over top of potatoes. Serves 4 to 6.

Cheesy Ranch Potatoes

- **2½ pounds new (red) potatoes with peels, quartered**   910 g
- **1 onion, cut into 8 wedges**
- **1 (10 ounce) can fiesta nacho cheese soup**   280 g
- **1 (8 ounce) carton sour cream**   225 g
- **1 (1 ounce) packet ranch salad dressing mix**   30 g
- **Chopped fresh parsley**

Place potatoes and onion in sprayed 4 to 5-quart (4 to 5 L) slow cooker.

Combine, nacho cheese soup, sour cream and dressing mix in bowl and whisk well to mix. Spoon over potato-onion mixture.

Cover and cook on LOW for 6 to 7 hours. To serve, sprinkle parsley over potato mixture. Serves 4 to 6.

Creamy Potatoes au Gratin

- 1 (10 ounce) can cheddar cheese soup   280 g
- ½ soup can milk
- 1 (8 ounce) package cream cheese   225 g
- 2 cloves garlic, minced
- 8 - 10 baking potatoes, peeled, thinly sliced, divided
- 3 onions, thinly sliced, divided

Combine soup, milk, cream cheese and garlic in large saucepan over low heat and stir until cream cheese melts.

Place half the potatoes and half the onions in sprayed slow cooker and season with a little salt and pepper.

Pour half cheese soup mixture over top. Place remaining potatoes and onions in slow cooker. Pour remaining cheese soup mixture over top.

Cover and cook on LOW for 6 to 7 hours or until potatoes are tender and liquid is almost gone. Sprinkle cheddar cheese over top and cook on HIGH for about 10 minutes. Serves 4 to 6.

Diced Potato Blend

- **1 (28 ounce) bag frozen diced potatoes with onions and peppers, thawed**   **795 g**
- **1 onion, chopped**
- **1 bell pepper, cored, seeded, chopped**
- **2 ribs celery, chopped**
- **1 (8 ounce) package shredded Monterey Jack-cheddar cheese blend**   **225 g**
- **1 (10 ounce) can cream of celery soup**   **280 g**
- **1 (8 ounce) carton sour cream**   **225 g**

Combine potatoes, onion, bell pepper, celery, cheese, soup, sour cream and 1 teaspoon (5 ml) pepper in sprayed 5 to 6-quart (5 to 6 L) slow cooker and mix well.

Cover and cook on LOW 4 to 6 hours. Stir well before serving. Serves 6 to 8.

Brown-Sugar Topped Sweet Potatoes

• 3 (15 ounce) cans sweet potatoes, drained	3 (425 g)
• ½ (20 ounce) can pineapple pie filling	½ (570 g)
• 2 tablespoons butter, melted	30 g
• ½ cup packed brown sugar	110 g
• ½ teaspoon ground cinnamon	2 ml

Place sweet potatoes, pie filling, melted butter, brown sugar and cinnamon in sprayed 4 to 5-quart (4 to 5 L) slow cooker and lightly stir.

Cover and cook on LOW for 2 to 3 hours. Serves 6 to 8.

Topping:

• 1 cup packed light brown sugar	220 g
• 3 tablespoons butter, melted	40 g
• ½ cup flour	60 g
• 1 cup coarsely chopped nuts	110 g

While potatoes cook, combine topping ingredients in bowl, spread out on foil-lined baking pan and bake at 350° (175° C) for 15 to 20 minutes.

When ready to serve, sprinkle topping over sweet potatoes.

Glazed Sweet Potatoes

• 3 (15 ounce) cans sweet potatoes, drained	3 (425 g)
• ¼ cup (½ stick) butter, melted	60 g
• 2 cups packed brown sugar	440 g
• ⅓ cup orange juice	75 ml
• ½ teaspoon ground cinnamon	2 ml

After draining sweet potatoes, cut into smaller chunks and place in 4 to 5-quart (4 to 5 L) slow cooker.

Add butter, brown sugar, orange juice, a little salt and a sprinkle of cinnamon and stir well. Cover and cook on LOW for 4 to 5 hours. Serves 4 to 6.

Spicy Spanish Rice

• 1½ cups white rice	280 g
• 1 (10 ounce) can diced tomatoes and green chilies	280 g
• 1 (15 ounce) can stewed tomatoes	425 g
• 1 (1 ounce) packet taco seasoning	30 g
• 1 large onion, chopped	

Combine all ingredients plus 2 cups (500 ml) water in sprayed 5-quart (5 L) slow cooker and stir well.

Cover and cook on LOW for 5 to 7 hours. (The flavor will go through the rice better if you stir 2 or 3 times during cooking time.) Serves 4.

TIP: Make this "a main dish" by slicing 1 pound (455 g) Polish sausage slices to rice mixture.

Delicious Risotto Rice

- 1½ cups Italian risotto rice — 280 g
- 3 (14 ounce) cans chicken broth — 3 (395 g)
- 3 tablespoons butter, melted — 40 g
- 1½ cups sliced, fresh mushrooms — 110 g
- 1 cup sliced celery — 100 g

Combine rice, broth, butter, mushrooms and celery in sprayed 4 to 5-quart (4 to 5 L) slow cooker.

Cover and cook on LOW for 2 to 3 hours or until rice is tender. Serves 4 to 6.

Crunchy Couscous

When rice is boring, try couscous.

- 1 (10 ounce) box original plain couscous — 280 g
- 2 cups sliced celery — 200 g
- 1 red bell pepper, seeded, chopped
- 1 yellow bell pepper, seeded, chopped
- 1 (16 ounce) jar creamy alfredo sauce — 455 g

Combine couscous, celery, bell peppers, alfredo sauce and 1½ cups (375 ml) water in sprayed 5-quart (5 L) slow cooker and mix well.

Cover and cook on LOW for 2 hours, stir once or twice.

Check slow cooker to make sure celery and peppers are cooked, but still crunchy. Serves 4 to 6.

Herbed-Chicken Couscous

- 1 (5.7 ounce) box herbed-chicken couscous   **155 g**
- 1 red bell pepper, julienned
- 1 green bell pepper, julienned
- 2 small yellow squash, sliced
- 1 (16 ounce) package frozen mixed vegetables, thawed   **455 g**
- 1 (10 ounce) can French onion soup   **280 g**
- ¼ cup (½ stick) butter, melted   **60 g**
- ½ teaspoon seasoned salt   **2 ml**

Combine all ingredients with 1½ cups (375 ml) water in sprayed slow cooker and mix well.

Cover and cook on LOW for 2 to 4 hours. Serves 4.

Cheese-Spaghetti and Spinach

• 1 (7 ounce) box ready-cut spaghetti	**200 g**
• 2 tablespoons butter	**30 g**
• 1 (8 ounce) carton sour cream	**225 g**
• 1 cup shredded cheddar cheese	**115 g**
• 1 (8 ounce) package Monterey Jack cheese, divided	**225 g**
• 1 (12 ounce) package frozen, chopped spinach, thawed, well drained*	**340 g**
• 1 (6 ounce) can cheddar french-fried onions, divided	**170 g**

Cook spaghetti according to package directions, drain and stir in butter until it melts.

Combine sour cream, cheddar cheese, half Monterey Jack cheese, spinach and half can onions in large bowl.

Fold into spaghetti and spoon into sprayed slow cooker. Cover and cook on LOW for 2 to 4 hours.

When ready to serve, sprinkle remaining Jack cheese and fried onion rings over top. Serves 4.

*TIP: Squeeze spinach between paper towels to completely remove excess moisture.

Creamy Spinach with Noodles

- 1 (12 ounce) package medium noodles   340 g
- 1 cup half-and-half cream   250 ml
- 1 (10 ounce) package frozen chopped spinach, thawed   280 g
- 6 tablespoons (¾ stick) butter, melted   85 g
- 2 teaspoons seasoned salt   10 ml
- 1½ cups shredded cheddar-Monterey Jack cheese   170 g

Cook noodles according to package directions and drain.

Place in sprayed 5 to 6-quart (5 to 6 L) slow cooker. Add half-and-half cream, spinach, butter and seasoned salt and stir until they blend well.

Cover and cook on LOW for 2 to 3 hours. When ready to serve, fold in cheese. Serves 4.

Macaroni and Cheese

- 4 cups cooked macaroni, drained   560 g
- 2 tablespoons butter, melted   30 g
- 1 onion, minced
- 2 cups evaporated milk   500 ml
- 2 cups shredded cheddar cheese   225 g
- 1 cup shredded colby or Monterey Jack cheese   115 g

Mix macaroni and butter in sprayed slow cooker. Add onion and milk and stir to blend. Add cheeses and stir well. Cover and cook on LOW for 2 to 3 hours. Serves 4 to 6.

Chicken
& Turkey
Main Dishes

Simple Chicken Dinner

- **6 - 8 boneless, skinless chicken breast halves**
- **2 onions, sliced**
- **3 potatoes, peeled, sliced**
- **1 (8 ounce) package baby carrots**   **225 g**
- **1 teaspoon parsley flakes**   **5 ml**
- **½ teaspoon cayenne pepper**   **2 ml**
- **1 (15 ounce) can stewed tomatoes with liquid**   **425 g**
- **Rice, cooked**

Season chicken breasts with a little salt and pepper. Sear outside of chicken breasts in sprayed skillet. Place vegetables in sprayed slow cooker and place chicken breasts on top. Sprinkle parsley flakes, cayenne, and a little salt and pepper over chicken.

Pour tomatoes over chicken. Cover and cook on LOW for 6 to 8 hours. Serve over cooked rice. Serves 6 to 8.

Recipes in this cookbook may be cooked in 3 to 6-quart slow cookers. You may need to adjust the quantity of ingredients for a smaller cooker.

Chicken Breasts with Rice

- 1¾ cups flour   210 g
- Scant 2 tablespoons dry mustard   30 ml
- 6 boneless, skinless chicken breast halves
- 2 tablespoons canola oil   30 ml
- 1 (10 ounce) can chicken-rice soup   280 g
- 2 ribs celery, chopped

Place flour and mustard in shallow bowl and dredge chicken to coat all sides.
Brown chicken breasts in oil in skillet. Place all breasts in sprayed 6-quart (6 L)
oval slow cooker.

Pour chicken, soup and celery over chicken and add about ¼ cup (60 ml)
water. Cover and cook on LOW for 6 to 7 hours. Serves 4 to 6.

Easy Apricot Chicken

- 6 boneless, skinless chicken breast halves
- 1 (12 ounce) jar apricot preserves   340 g
- 1 (8 ounce) bottle Catalina dressing   235 ml
- 1 (1 ounce) packet onion soup mix   30 g

Place chicken in sprayed 6-quart (6 L) slow cooker. Combine apricot preserves,
Catalina dressing, onion soup mix and ¼ cup (60 ml) water and stir well.

Cover chicken breasts with sauce mixture. Cover and cook on LOW for 5 to
6 hours. Serves 4 to 6.

Artichoke Chicken

- 1 (14 ounce) can artichoke hearts, drained   395 g
- 1 (12 ounce) package mushrooms, stemmed   340 g
- ¾ cup white wine   175 ml
- ½ cup balsamic vinaigrette   125 ml
- 6 boneless, skinless, chicken breast halves
- 1 (6 ounce) jar marinated artichokes with liquid   170 g

Place artichoke hearts in slow cooker with half of mushrooms. In separate bowl, mix white wine and vinaigrette.

Place chicken breasts in cooker. Pour wine mixture over chicken. Add marinated artichokes and remaining mushrooms.

Cook on LOW for about 5 hours or until juices in chicken are clear. Serves 4 to 6.

Artichoke-Chicken Pasta

- 1½ pounds boneless, skinless chicken breast tenders   680 g
- 1 (15 ounce) can artichoke hearts, quartered   425 g
- ¾ cup chopped, roasted, red peppers   110 g
- 1 (8 ounce) package American cheese, shredded   225 g
- 1 tablespoon marinade for chicken   15 ml
- 1 (10 ounce) can cream of chicken soup   280 g
- 1 (8 ounce) package shredded cheddar cheese   225 g
- 4 cups hot, cooked bow-tie pasta   300 g

Combine chicken tenders, artichoke, roasted peppers, American cheese, marinade for chicken and soup in sprayed slow cooker and mix well.

Cover and cook on LOW for 6 to 8 hours. About 20 minutes before serving, fold in cheddar cheese, hot pasta and a little salt and pepper. Serves 4.

Cooking time on HIGH equals about half the cooking time on LOW.

Broccoli-Rice Chicken

- 1¼ cups converted rice   250 g
- 2 pounds boneless, skinless chicken breast halves   680 g
- Dried parsley
- 1 (2 ounce) packet cream of broccoli soup mix   60 g
- 1 (14 ounce) can chicken broth   395 g

Place rice in sprayed slow cooker. Cut chicken into slices and place over rice. Sprinkle with parsley and a little pepper.

Combine soup mix, chicken broth and 1 cup (250 ml) water in saucepan. Heat just enough to mix well. Pour over chicken and rice.

Cover and cook on LOW for 6 to 8 hours. Serves 4 to 6.

Bacon-Wrapped Chicken

- 1 (2.5 ounce) jar dried beef   70 g
- 6 boneless, skinless chicken breast halves
- 6 slices bacon
- 2 (10 ounce) cans golden mushroom soup   2 (280 g)
- 1 (6 ounce) package parmesan-butter rice, cooked   170 g

Place dried beef sliced in sprayed 5-quart (5 L) slow cooker. Roll each chicken breast half in slice of bacon and place over dried beef.

Heat soup and ⅓ cup (75 ml) water in saucepan just enough to mix well and pour over chicken.

Cover and cook on LOW for 7 to 8 hours. Serve over rice. Serves 4 to 6.

Purchase a slow cooker that has a removable ceramic insert; it is easier to clean. Allow it to cool completely before washing or soaking. With most models, the removable bowl can be used as a ready-to-go serving dish.

Broccoli-Cheese Chicken

- 4 boneless, skinless chicken breast halves
- 2 tablespoons butter, melted — 30 g
- 1 (10 ounce) can broccoli-cheese soup — 280 g
- ¼ cup milk — 60 ml
- 1 (10 ounce) package frozen broccoli spears — 280 g
- Rice, cooked

Dry chicken breasts with paper towels and place in sprayed, oval slow cooker.

Combine melted butter, soup and milk in bowl and spoon over chicken. Cover and cook on LOW for 4 to 6 hours.

Remove cooker lid and place broccoli over chicken. Cover and cook for additional 1 hour. Serve over rice. Serves 4.

Creamy Smothered Chicken

- 2 tablespoons butter, melted — 30 g
- 4 boneless, skinless chicken breast halves
- 1 (10 ounce) can cream of mushroom soup — 280 g
- 2 tablespoons dry Italian salad dressing — 30 ml
- ½ cup sherry — 125 ml
- 1 (8 ounce) package cream cheese, cubed — 225 g
- Noodles, cooked

Brush melted butter over chicken breasts.

Place in sprayed, oval slow cooker and add remaining ingredients. Cover and cook on LOW for 6 to 7 hours. Serve over noodles. Serves 4.

> *Because the lid forms a seal with the slow cooker, there is very little evaporation of the cooking liquid. If a stovetop recipe is converted to the slow cooker method, the amount of liquid used (water, broth, etc.) should be reduced. Liquid can be added later if needed.*

Chicken and Noodles

- **2 pounds boneless, skinless chicken breast halves**　　910 g
- **¼ cup cornstarch**　　30 g
- **⅓ cup soy sauce**　　75 ml
- **2 onions, chopped**
- **3 ribs celery, sliced diagonally**
- **1 red bell pepper, seeded, julienned**
- **2 (14 ounce) cans mixed Chinese vegetables, drained**　　2 (395 g)
- **¼ cup molasses**　　60 ml
- **2 cups chow mein noodles**　　110 g

Place chicken breasts and 2 cups (500 ml) water in sprayed slow cooker. Cover and cook on LOW for 3 to 4 hours.

At least 1 hour before serving, remove chicken and cut into bite-size pieces. Combine cornstarch and soy sauce in bowl and mix well. Stir into slow cooker.

Add onions, celery, bell pepper, mixed vegetables and molasses. Cover and cook on HIGH heat for 1 to 2 hours.

Serve over chow mein noodles. Serves 4 to 6.

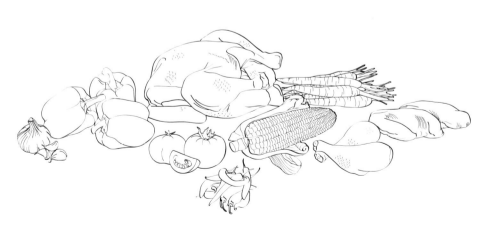

Chicken and Pasta

- 1 (16 ounce) package frozen whole green beans, thawed   **455 g**
- 1 onion, chopped
- 1 cup fresh mushroom halves   **70 g**
- 3 boneless, skinless chicken breast halves
- 1 (15 ounce) can Italian stewed tomatoes   **425 g**
- 1 teaspoon chicken bouillon granules   **5 ml**
- 1 teaspoon minced garlic   **5 ml**
- 1 teaspoon Italian seasoning   **5 ml**
- 1 (8 ounce) package fettuccini   **225 g**
- 1 (4 ounce) package grated parmesan cheese   **115 g**

Place green beans, onion and mushrooms in sprayed 4-quart (4 L) slow cooker.

Cut chicken into 1-inch (2.5 cm) pieces and place over vegetables.

Combine stewed tomatoes, chicken bouillon, garlic and Italian seasoning in small bowl. Pour over chicken.

Cover and cook on LOW for 5 to 6 hours. Cook fettuccini according to package directions and drain.

Serve chicken over fettuccini sprinkled with parmesan cheese. Serves 4.

TIP: Add ¼ cup (60 g) butter to make this dish have a richer taste.

Chicken-Vegetable Mix

- 4 - 5 boneless, skinless chicken breast halves
- 2 teaspoons seasoned salt   10 ml
- 1 (16 ounce) package frozen broccoli, cauliflower and
  carrots, thawed   455 g
- 1 (10 ounce) can cream of celery soup   280 g
- 1 (8 ounce) package shredded cheddar- Jack cheese, divided 225 g

Cut chicken into strips, sprinkle with seasoned salt and place in sprayed slow cooker.

Combine vegetables, celery soup and half cheese in large bowl and mix well. Spoon over chicken breasts.

Cover and cook on LOW for 4 to 5 hours. About 10 minutes before serving, sprinkle remaining cheese on top of casserole. Serves 4 to 6.

Chicken Curry over Rice

- 3 large boneless, skinless chicken breast halves
- ½ cup chicken broth   125 ml
- 1 (10 ounce) can cream of chicken soup   280 g
- 1 onion, coarsely chopped
- 1 red bell pepper, seeded, julienned
- ¼ cup golden raisins   40 g
- 1½ teaspoons curry powder   7 ml
- ¼ teaspoon ground ginger   1 ml
- Rice, cooked

Cut chicken into thin strips and place in sprayed 5 to 6-quart (5 to 6 L) slow cooker.

Combine broth, soup, onion, bell pepper, raisins, curry powder and ginger in bowl and mix well. Pour over chicken.

Cover and cook on LOW for 3 to 4 hours. Serve over rice. Serves 4.

Chicken Delicious

- 5 - 6 boneless skinless chicken breast halves
- 1 (16 ounce) package frozen broccoli florets, thawed   455 g
- 1 red bell pepper, seeded, julienned
- 1 (16 ounce) jar Cheesy Ragu® Roasted Garlic Parmesan sauce   455 g
- 3 tablespoons sherry   45 ml
- Noodles, cooked

Brown chicken breasts in skillet and place in sprayed 5 to 6-quart (5 to 6 L) oval slow cooker.

Place broccoli florets on plate, remove much of stem and discard.

Combine broccoli florets, bell pepper, cheese sauce and sherry in bowl and mix well. Spoon over chicken breasts.

Cover and cook on LOW for 4 to 5 hours. Serve over noodles. Serves 4 to 6.

Chicken Breast Roll-Ups

- 6 boneless, skinless chicken breast halves
- 1 cup ricotta cheese   245 g
- ½ cup shredded parmesan cheese   50 g
- ½ cup prepared pesto sauce   115 g
- ½ (10 ounce) can cream of mushroom soup   ½ (280 g)
- ¼ cup milk   60 ml
- ¼ cup wine   60 ml

Pound chicken breast halves to about ½-inch thick. Mix ricotta cheese, pesto and parmesan in bowl. Divide ricotta mixture among chicken breasts and roll up each. Secure with toothpick and place in sprayed slow cooker.

In small saucepan, mix soup, milk and wine over low heat until combined. Pour over chicken. Cover and cook on LOW about 6 hours or until chicken juices are clear. Serves 6.

Chicken in Celery Sauce

- ¾ cup white rice   150 g
- 1 (14 ounce) can chicken broth   395 g
- 1 (1 ounce) packet onion soup mix   30 g
- 1 red bell pepper, seeded, chopped
- 2 ribs celery, chopped
- 1 onion, chopped
- 2 (10 ounce) cans cream of celery soup   2 (280 g)
- ¾ cup white cooking wine   175 ml
- 4 - 6 boneless skinless chicken breast halves
- 1 (3 ounce) package grated fresh parmesan cheese   85 g

Combine rice, broth, soup mix, bell pepper, celery, onion, celery soup, ¾ cup (175 ml) water, wine and several sprinkles of black pepper in bowl and mix well. (Make sure to mix soup well with liquids.)

Place chicken breasts in sprayed 6-quart (6 L) oval slow cooker. Pour rice-soup mixture over chicken breasts. Cover and cook on LOW for 4 to 6 hours.

One hour before serving, sprinkle parmesan cheese over chicken. Serves 4 to 6.

Chicken thighs are more flavorful and less likely to overcook than chicken breasts in slow cooker recipes.

Chicken Fajitas

- **2 pounds boneless, skinless chicken breast halves**   **910 g**
- **1 onion, thinly sliced**
- **1 red bell pepper, cored, seeded, julienned**
- **1 teaspoon ground cumin**   **5 ml**
- **2 teaspoons chili powder**   **7 ml**
- **1 tablespoon lime juice**   **15 ml**
- **½ cup chicken broth**   **125 ml**
- **8 - 10 warm flour tortillas**
- **Guacamole**
- **Sour cream**
- **Lettuce and tomatoes**

Cut chicken into diagonal strips and place in sprayed slow cooker. Top with onion and bell pepper.

Combine cumin, chili powder, lime juice and chicken broth in bowl and pour over chicken and vegetables. Cover and cook on LOW for 5 to 7 hours.

Serve several slices of chicken mixture with sauce into center of each warm tortilla and fold.

Serve with guacamole, sour cream, lettuce or tomatoes or plain. Serves 4 to 6.

Cooking time on HIGH equals about half the cooking time on LOW.

Salsa Chicken Fajitas

- **4 boneless, skinless chicken breast halves**
- **1 (1 ounce) packet taco seasoning**   **30 g**
- **2 tablespoons flour**   **15 g**
- **1 cup chunky salsa**   **265 g**
- **1 green bell pepper, seeded, sliced**
- **1 red bell pepper, seeded, sliced**
- **1 large onion, sliced**
- **1 (8 ounce) package shredded cheddar cheese**   **225 g**
- **8 flour tortillas**

Season chicken breasts with taco seasoning, dredge in flour and brown in hot oil in skillet. Drain and place in sprayed slow cooker.

Pour salsa over chicken, cover and cook on LOW for about 6 hours. Slice chicken in ½-inch (1.3 cm) strips and return to slow cooker.

Turn slow cooker to HIGH, add bell peppers and onions and cook for 1 more hour or until vegetables are tender and chicken juices are clear.

Serve with shredded cheese and warm tortillas. Serves 4 to 6.

Chicken with Green Beans and New Potatoes

- 5 - 6 boneless, skinless chicken breast halves
- 6 carrots, peeled, cut in 1-inch length   6 (2.5 cm)
- 1 onion, chopped
- 1 (15 ounce) can cut green beans, drained   425 g
- 1 (15 ounce) can whole new potatoes, drained   425 g
- 2 (10 ounce) cans cream of mushroom soup   2 (280 g)
- Shredded cheddar cheese

Place chicken breasts in sprayed, oval slow cooker.

Combine, carrots, green beans, potatoes and mushroom soup in bowl and pour over chicken in cooker.

Cover and cook on LOW for 8 to 10 hours. When ready to serve, sprinkle cheese over top. Serves 4 to 6.

Chicken Ready

- 1 (6 ounce) package stuffing mix   170 g
- 3 cups cooked, chopped chicken breasts   420 g
- 1 (16 ounce) package frozen whole green beans, thawed   455 g
- 2 (12 ounce) jars chicken gravy   2 (340 g)

Prepare stuffing mix according to package directions and place in sprayed, oval slow cooker.

Follow with layer of cooked chicken and place green beans over chicken. Pour chicken gravy over green beans.

Cover and cook on LOW for 3 hours 30 minutes to 4 hours. Serves 4 to 6.

While reheating leftovers in a slow cooker is not recommended, the ceramic insert is usually ovenproof as well as microwaveable. Check the manufacturer's directions.

Chicken Marseilles

- **4 - 5 boneless, skinless chicken breast halves**
- **2 tablespoons butter**   **30 g**
- **1 (2 ounce) packet leek soup and dip mix**   **60 g**
- **½ teaspoon dill weed**   **2 ml**
- **1 cup milk**   **250 ml**
- **Brown rice, cooked**
- **¾ cup sour cream**   **180 g**

Place chicken breasts in sprayed, large slow cooker.

Combine butter, leek soup mix, dill weed, milk and ½ cup (125 ml) water in saucepan and heat just enough for butter to melt and ingredients to mix well. Pour over chicken.

Cover and cook on LOW for 3 to 5 hours.

When ready to serve, remove chicken breasts to platter with hot, cooked brown rice and cover to keep warm.

Add sour cream to cooker liquid and stir well. Pour sauce over chicken and rice. Serves 4 to 5.

Chicken Breasts Deluxe

- **4 slices bacon**
- **5 - 6 boneless, skinless chicken breast halves**
- **1 cup sliced celery**   100 g
- **1 cup sliced red bell pepper**   90 g
- **1 (10 ounce) can cream of chicken soup**   280 g
- **2 tablespoons white wine or cooking wine**   30 ml
- **6 slices Swiss cheese**
- **2 tablespoons dried parsley**   30 ml

Cook bacon in large skillet, drain, crumble and reserve drippings. Place chicken in skillet with bacon drippings and lightly brown on both sides.

Transfer chicken to sprayed, oval slow cooker and place celery and bell pepper over chicken.

In same skillet, combine soup and wine, stir and spoon over vegetables and chicken. Cover and cook on LOW for 3 to 4 hours.

Top with slices of cheese over each chicken breast and add parsley. Cook for additional 10 minutes.

Serve with creamy sauce and sprinkle with crumbled bacon. Serves 4 to 6.

Chicken Alfredo

- **5 boneless, skinless chicken breast halves**
- **1 (16 ounce) jar alfredo sauce**   **455 g**
- **1 (16 ounce) package frozen green peas, thawed**   **455 g**
- **1½ cups shredded mozzarella cheese**   **170 g**
- **Noodles, cooked**

Cut chicken into strips and place in sprayed slow cooker. Combine alfredo sauce, peas and cheese in bowl and mix well. Spoon over chicken strips.

Cover and cook on LOW for 5 to 6 hours. When ready to serve, spoon over noodles. Serves 4 to 5.

Cream of Chicken with New Potatoes

- **6 medium new (red) potatoes with peels, quartered**
- **4 - 5 carrots**
- **4 - 5 boneless, skinless chicken breast halves**
- **1 tablespoon chicken seasoning**   **15 ml**
- **2 (10 ounce) cans cream of chicken soup**   **2 (280 g)**
- **⅓ cup white wine or cooking wine**   **75 ml**

Cut carrots into ½-inch (1.2 cm) pieces. Place potatoes and carrots in sprayed slow cooker.

Sprinkle chicken breasts with chicken seasoning and place over vegetables.

Heat soups, wine and ¼ cup (60 ml) water in saucepan just to mix and pour over chicken and vegetables.

Cover and cook on LOW for 5 to 6 hours. Serves 4 to 5.

TIP: Use 1 (10 ounce/280 g) can chicken soup and 1 (10 ounce/280 g) can mushroom soup for a tasty change.

Easy Barbecued Chicken

- **6 boneless, skinless chicken breast halves**
- **½ cup flour** — **60 g**
- **½ cup orange marmalade** — **160 g**
- **½ cup ketchup** — **135 g**
- **¼ cup packed brown sugar** — **55 g**
- **⅓ cup soy sauce** — **75 ml**
- **1 tablespoon white wine vinegar** — **15 ml**
- **3 cloves garlic, minced**

Dredge chicken through flour and brown in skillet in a little hot oil over high heat. Drain and place in slow cooker.

In separate saucepan, cook marmalade, ketchup, brown sugar, soy sauce, vinegar and garlic over low heat just to mix well.

Pour over chicken and cook on LOW for 7 to 8 hours or until chicken juices run clear. Serves 6 to 8.

Chow Mein Chicken

- 4 boneless, skinless chicken breast halves
- 2 - 3 cups sliced celery   200 - 300 g
- 1 onion, coarsely chopped
- ⅓ cup soy sauce   75 ml
- ¼ teaspoon cayenne pepper   1 ml
- 1 (14 ounce) can chicken broth   395 g
- 1 (15 ounce) can bean sprouts, drained   425 g
- 1 (8 ounce) can water chestnuts, drained   225 g
- 1 (6 ounce) can bamboo shoots   170 g
- ¼ cup flour   30 g
- Chow mein noodles

Combine chicken, celery, onion, soy sauce, cayenne pepper and chicken broth in sprayed slow cooker. Cover and cook on LOW for 3 to 4 hours.

Add bean sprouts, water chestnuts and bamboo shoots to chicken. Mix flour and ¼ cup (60 ml) water in bowl and stir into chicken and vegetables.

Cook for additional 1 hour. Serve over chow mein noodles. Serves 4.

Chicken Creation

- 1 (6 ounce) box long grain-wild rice mix   170 g
- 1 (16 ounce) jar Cheesy Ragu® Roasted Garlic Parmesan sauce   455 g
- 12 - 15 frozen chicken breast tenderloins, thawed
- 1 cup frozen petite green peas, thawed   145 g

Pour 2½ cups (625 ml) water, rice and seasoning packet in sprayed 5-quart (5 L) slow cooker and stir well.

Spoon in cheese sauce and mix well. Place chicken tenderloins in slow cooker and cover with green peas.

Cover and cook on LOW for 4 to 5 hours. Serves 4.

Creamy Chicken and Potatoes

- 4 boneless, skinless chicken breast halves
- 2 teaspoons chicken seasoning   10 ml
- 8 - 10 small new (red) potatoes with peels
- 1 (10 ounce) can cream of chicken soup   280 g
- 1 (8 ounce) carton sour cream   225 g

Place chicken breast halves, sprinkled with chicken seasoning in sprayed slow cooker.

Arrange new potatoes around chicken. Combine soup, sour cream and good amount of pepper in bowl. Spoon over chicken breasts.

Cover and cook on LOW for 4 to 6 hours. Serves 4.

Cream Chicken

- Lemon juice
- 8 boneless, skinless chicken thighs
- 1 red bell pepper, seeded, chopped
- 2 ribs celery, sliced diagonally
- 1 (10 ounce) can cream of chicken soup   280 g
- 1 (10 ounce) can cream of celery soup   280 g
- ⅓ cup dry white wine   75 ml
- 1 (4 ounce) package grated parmesan cheese   115 g
- Rice

Rub a little lemon juice over chicken and sprinkle with a little salt and pepper.

Place in sprayed slow cooker and top with bell pepper and celery. Combine soups and wine in saucepan and heat just enough to mix thoroughly.

Pour over chicken breasts and sprinkle with parmesan cheese. Cover and cook on LOW for 6 to 7 hours. Serve over cooked rice. Serves 4 to 5.

Chicken and Vegetables

- 4 large boneless, skinless chicken breast halves
- 1 (10 ounce) can cream of chicken soup   280 g
- 1 (16 ounce) package frozen peas and carrots, thawed   455 g
- 1 (12 ounce) jar chicken gravy   340 g
- Buttermilk biscuits or Texas toast

Cut chicken in thin slices. Pour soup and ½ cup (125 ml) water into sprayed 6-quart (6 L) slow cooker, mix and add chicken slices.

Sprinkle a little salt and lots of pepper over chicken and soup. Cover and cook on LOW for 4 to 5 hours.

Add peas and carrots, chicken gravy and ½ cup (125 ml) water. Increase heat to HIGH and cook for about 1 hour or until peas and carrots are tender.

Serve over large, refrigerated buttermilk biscuits or over Texas toast (thick slices of bread). Serves 4.

Creamy Salsa Chicken

- 4 - 5 boneless, skinless chicken breast halves
- 1 (1 ounce) packet dry taco seasoning mix   30 g
- 1 cup salsa   265 g
- ½ cup sour cream   120 g

Place chicken breasts in sprayed 5 to 6-quart (5 to 6 L) slow cooker and add ¼ cup (60 ml) water.

Sprinkle taco seasoning mix over chicken and top with salsa. Cover and cook on LOW for 5 to 6 hours.

When ready to serve, remove chicken breasts and place on platter. Stir sour cream into salsa sauce and spoon over chicken breasts. Serves 4 to 5.

Chicken with Peas and Corn

- 8 boneless, skinless chicken thighs
- 1 (15 ounce) can whole kernel corn, drained   425 g
- 1 (10 ounce) box frozen green peas, thawed   280 g
- 1 (16 ounce) jar alfredo sauce   455 g
- 1 teaspoon chicken seasoning   5 ml
- 1 teaspoon minced garlic   5 ml
- Pasta, cooked

Brown chicken thighs in skillet and place in sprayed, oval slow cooker.

Combine corn, peas, alfredo sauce, ¼ cup (60 ml) water, chicken seasoning and minced garlic in bowl and spoon mixture over chicken breasts.

Cover and cook on LOW for 4 to 5 hours. Serve over pasta. Serves 4 to 5.

Slow Cooker Cordon Bleu

- 4 boneless, skinless chicken breast halves
- 4 slices cooked ham
- 4 slices Swiss cheese, softened
- 1 (10 ounce) can cream of chicken soup   280 g
- ¼ cup milk   60 ml
- Noodles, cooked

Place chicken breasts on cutting board and pound until breast halves are thin.

Place ham and cheese slices on chicken breasts, roll and secure with toothpick. Arrange chicken rolls in sprayed 4-quart (4 L) slow cooker.

Pour chicken soup with milk into saucepan, heat just enough to mix well and pour over chicken rolls. Cover and cook on LOW for 4 to 5 hours.

Serve over noodles and cover with sauce from soup. Serves 4.

Delicious Chicken Pasta

- **1 pound chicken tenders**   **455 g**
- **Lemon-herb chicken seasoning**
- **3 tablespoons butter**   **40 g**
- **1 onion, coarsely chopped**
- **1 (15 ounce) can diced tomatoes**   **425 g**
- **1 (10 ounce) can golden mushroom soup**   **280 g**
- **1 (8 ounce) box angel hair pasta**   **225 g**

Pat chicken tenders dry with several paper towels and sprinkle ample amount of chicken seasoning.

Melt butter in large skillet, brown chicken and place in sprayed, oval slow cooker. Pour remaining butter and seasonings over chicken and cover with onion.

Combine tomatoes and mushroom soup in bowl and pour over chicken and onions. Cover and cook on LOW for 4 to 5 hours.

When ready to serve, cook pasta according to package directions. Serve chicken and sauce over pasta. Serves 4.

Chicken thighs are more flavorful and less likely to overcook than chicken breasts in slow cooker recipes.

147

Farmhouse Supper

- **1 (8 ounce) package medium noodles**   **225 g**
- **4 - 5 boneless, skinless chicken breast halves**
- **Canola oil**
- **1 (14 ounce) can chicken broth**   **395 g**
- **2 cups sliced celery**   **200 g**
- **2 onions, chopped**
- **1 green bell pepper, seeded, chopped**
- **1 red bell pepper, seeded, chopped**
- **1 (10 ounce) can cream of chicken soup**   **280 g**
- **1 (10 ounce) can cream of mushroom soup**   **280 g**
- **1 cup shredded 4-cheese blend**   **115 g**

Cook noodles in boiling water until barely tender and drain well. Cut chicken into thin slices and brown lightly in skillet with a little oil

Mix noodles, chicken and broth in sprayed, large slow cooker. Make sure noodles separate and coat with broth. Stir in remaining ingredients.

Cover and cook on LOW for 4 to 6 hours. Serves 4 to 5.

Golden Chicken Dinner

- 5 boneless, skinless chicken breast halves
- 6 medium new (red) potatoes with peels, cubed
- 6 medium carrots, chopped
- 1 tablespoon dried parsley flakes   15 ml
- 1 teaspoon seasoned salt   5 ml
- 1 (10 ounce) can golden mushroom soup   280 g
- 1 (10 ounce) can cream of chicken soup   280 g
- ¼ cup dried mashed potato flakes   15 g

Cut chicken into ½-inch (1.2 cm) pieces. Place potatoes and carrots in sprayed slow cooker and top with chicken breasts.

Sprinkle parsley flakes, seasoned salt and ½ teaspoon (2 ml) pepper over chicken. Combine soups in bowl and spread over chicken. Cover and cook on LOW for 6 to 7 hours.

Stir in potato flakes and a little water or milk if necessary to make gravy and cook for additional 30 minutes. Serves 4 to 6.

Hawaiian Chicken

- 6 boneless, skinless chicken breast halves
- 1 (15 ounce) can pineapple slices with juice   425 g
- ⅓ cup packed brown sugar   75 g
- 2 tablespoons lemon juice   30 ml
- ¼ teaspoon ground ginger   1 ml
- ¼ cup cornstarch   30 g
- Rice, cooked

Place chicken breasts in sprayed, oval slow cooker and sprinkle with a little salt. Place pineapple slices over chicken.

Combine pineapple juice, brown sugar, lemon juice, ginger and cornstarch in small bowl and stir until cornstarch mixes with liquids. Pour over chicken breasts.

Cover and cook on LOW for 4 to 5 hours or on HIGH for 2 hours 30 minutes to 3 hours. Serve over rice. Serves 4 to 6.

Imperial Chicken

- **1 (6 ounce) box long grain-wild rice mix**   **170 g**
- **1 (16 ounce) jar Cheesy Ragu® Roasted Garlic Parmesan sauce**   **455 g**
- **6 boneless, skinless chicken breast halves**
- **1 (16 ounce) box frozen French-style green beans, thawed**   **455 g**
- **½ cup slivered almonds, toasted**   **85 g**

Combine 2½ cups (625 ml) water, rice and seasoning packet into sprayed, oval slow cooker and stir well.

Spoon in cheese sauce and mix well. Place chicken breasts in slow cooker and cover with green beans.

Cover and cook on LOW for 3 to 5 hours. When ready to serve, sprinkle with slivered almonds. Serves 4 to 6.

Chicken with Stuffing

- **5 boneless, skinless chicken breast halves**
- **2 (10 ounce) cans cream of chicken soup**   **2 (280 g)**
- **1 (6 ounce) box chicken stuffing mix**   **170 g**
- **1 (16 ounce) package frozen green peas, thawed**   **455 g**

Place chicken breasts in sprayed 6-quart (6 L) slow cooker and spoon soups over chicken.

Combine stuffing mix with ingredients on package directions in bowl and spoon over chicken and soup.

Cover and cook on LOW for 5 to 6 hours.

Sprinkle drained green peas over top of stuffing. Cover and cook for additional 45 to 50 minutes. Serves 4 to 5.

TIP: Use 1 (10 ounce/280 g) can cream of chicken soup and 1 (10 ounce/280 g) can fiesta nacho soup for a nice variation.

Mushroom Chicken

- **4 boneless, skinless chicken breast halves**
- **1 (15 ounce) can tomato sauce**   **425 g**
- **2 (4 ounce) cans sliced mushrooms, drained**   **2 (115 g)**
- **1 (10 ounce) package frozen seasoning blend chopped onions and peppers**   **280 g**
- **2 teaspoons Italian seasoning**   **10 ml**
- **1 teaspoon minced garlic**   **5 ml**

Brown chicken breasts in skillet and place in sprayed, oval slow cooker.

Combine tomato sauce, mushrooms, onions and peppers, Italian seasoning, garlic and ¼ cup (60 ml) water in bowl and spoon over chicken breasts.

Cover and cook on LOW for 4 to 5 hours. Serves 4.

Orange Chicken

- 6 boneless, skinless chicken breast halves
- 1 (12 ounce) jar orange marmalade — 340 g
- 1 (8 ounce) bottle Russian salad dressing — 235 ml
- 1 (1 ounce) packet onion soup mix — 30 g

Place chicken breasts in sprayed, oval slow cooker. Combine orange marmalade, dressing, soup mix and ¾ cup (175 ml) water in bowl and stir well.

Spoon mixture over chicken breasts. Cover and cook on LOW for 4 to 6 hours. Serves 4 to 6.

Oregano Chicken

- ½ cup (1 stick) butter, melted — 115 g
- 1 (1 ounce) packet Italian salad dressing mix — 30 g
- 1 tablespoon lemon juice — 15 ml
- 4 - 5 boneless, skinless chicken breast halves
- 2 tablespoons dried oregano — 30 ml

Combine butter, dressing and lemon juice in bowl and mix well. Place chicken breasts in sprayed, large slow cooker. Spoon butter-lemon juice mixture over chicken. Cover and cook on LOW for 5 to 6 hours.

One hour before serving, baste chicken with pan juices and sprinkle oregano over chicken. Serves 4 to 6.

Quick-Fix Chicken

- **4 - 6 boneless, skinless chicken breast halves**
- **1 (8 ounce) carton sour cream**   **225 g**
- **¼ cup soy sauce**   **60 ml**
- **2 (10 ounce) cans French onion soup**   **2 (280 g)**
- **Rice or mashed potatoes, cooked**

Place chicken in sprayed, oval slow cooker.

Combine sour cream, soy sauce and onion soup in bowl, stir and mix well. Add to slow cooker

Cover and cook on LOW for 5 to 6 hours if chicken breasts are large, 3 to 4 hours if breasts are medium. Serves 4 to 6.

TIP: Serve chicken and sauce with hot, buttered rice or mashed potatoes.

Perfect Chicken Breasts

- **1 (2.5 ounce) jar dried beef**   **70 g**
- **6 small boneless, skinless chicken breast halves**
- **6 slices bacon**
- **2 (10 ounce) cans golden mushroom soup**   **2 (280 g)**

Line slices of dried beef in sprayed, oval slow cooker and overlap some.

Roll each chicken breast with slice of bacon and secure with toothpick. Place in slow cooker, overlapping as little as possible.

Combine mushroom soup and ½ cup (125 ml) water or milk in bowl and spoon over chicken breasts.

Cover and cook on LOW for 6 to 8 hours. Serves 4 to 6.

TIP: When cooked, you will have a great "gravy" that is wonderful served over noodles or rice.

Picante Chicken

- **4 boneless, skinless chicken breast halves**
- **1 green bell pepper, seeded, cut in rings**
- **1 (16 ounce) jar picante sauce**   **455 g**
- **⅓ cup packed brown sugar**   **75 g**
- **1 tablespoon mustard**   **15 ml**

Place chicken breasts in sprayed slow cooker with bell pepper rings over top of chicken.

Combine picante, brown sugar and mustard in bowl and spoon over top of chicken. Cover and cook on LOW for 4 to 5 hours. Serves 4.

Russian Chicken

- **1 (8 ounce) bottle Russian salad dressing**   **235 ml**
- **1 (16 ounce) can whole cranberry sauce**   **455 g**
- **1 (1 ounce) packet onion soup mix**   **30 g**
- **4 chicken quarters, skinned**
- **Rice, cooked**

Combine salad dressing, cranberry sauce, ½ cup (125 ml) water and soup mix in bowl. Stir well to get all lumps out of soup mix.

Place 4 chicken pieces in sprayed 6-quart (6 L) oval slow cooker and spoon dressing-cranberry mixture over chicken.

Cover and cook on LOW for 4 to 5 hours. Serve sauce and chicken over rice. Serves 4 to 6.

TIP: Use 6 chicken breasts if you don't want to cut-up a chicken.

Some flavors, such as chili powder and garlic, will become more intense during cooking. Others tend to "cook out" and lose their flavor. It is always wise to taste at the end of cooking and season as needed.

So-Good Chicken

- **4 - 5 boneless, skinless chicken breast halves**
- **1 (10 ounce) can golden mushroom soup**   **280 g**
- **1 cup white cooking wine**   **250 ml**
- **1 (8 ounce) carton sour cream**   **225 g**

Place chicken breasts in sprayed slow cooker and sprinkle a little salt and pepper over each.

Combine mushroom soup, wine and sour cream in bowl and mix well. Spoon over chicken breasts.

Cover and cook on LOW for 5 to 7 hours. Serves 4 to 6.

Winter Dinner

- **1 pound chicken tenderloins**   **455 g**
- **Canola oil**
- **1 pound Polish sausage, cut in 1-inch pieces**   **455 g/2.5 cm**
- **2 onions, chopped**
- **1 (28 ounce) can pork and beans with liquid**   **795 g**
- **1 (15 ounce) can ranch-style beans, drained**   **425 g**
- **1 (15 ounce) can great northern beans**   **425 g**
- **1 (15 ounce) can butter beans, drained**   **425 g**
- **1 cup ketchup**   **270 g**
- **1 cup packed brown sugar**   **220 g**
- **1 tablespoon vinegar**   **15 ml**
- **6 slices bacon, cooked, crumbled**

Brown chicken slices in a little oil in skillet and place in sprayed, large slow cooker. Add sausage, onions, 4 cans beans, ketchup, brown sugar and vinegar and stir gently.

Cover and cook on LOW for 7 to 8 hours or on HIGH for 3 hours 30 minutes to 4 hours. When ready to serve, sprinkle crumbled bacon over top. Serves 4 to 6.

Savory Chicken Fettuccini

- **2 pounds boneless, skinless chicken thighs, cubed**   910 g
- **½ teaspoon garlic powder**   2 ml
- **1 red bell pepper, seeded, chopped**
- **2 ribs celery, chopped**
- **1 (10 ounce) can cream of celery soup**   280 g
- **1 (10 ounce) can cream of chicken soup**   280 g
- **1 (8 ounce) package cubed Velveeta® cheese**   225 g
- **1 (4 ounce) jar diced pimentos**   115 g
- **1 (16 ounce) package spinach fettuccini**   455 g

Place cubed chicken pieces in sprayed slow cooker. Sprinkle with garlic powder, ½ teaspoon (2 ml) pepper, bell pepper and celery. Top with soups.

Cover and cook on HIGH for 4 to 6 hours or until chicken juices are clear. Stir in cheese and pimentos. Cover and cook until cheese melts.

Cook fettuccini according to package directions and drain. Place fettuccini in serving bowl and spoon chicken over fettuccini. Serve hot. Serves 4 to 6.

Recipes in this cookbook may be cooked in 3 to 6-quart slow cookers. You may need to adjust the quantity of ingredients for a smaller cooker.

Scrumptious Chicken Breasts

There is a lot of delicious sauce.

• **5 - 6 boneless, skinless chicken breast halves**	
• **1 teaspoon chicken seasoning**	**5 ml**
• **1 (10 ounce) can cream of chicken soup**	**280 g**
• **1 (10 ounce) can broccoli-cheese soup**	**280 g**
• **½ cup white cooking wine**	**125 ml**
• **Noodles, cooked**	

Place breast halves, sprinkled with pepper and chicken seasoning in sprayed, oval slow cooker.

Combine soups and wine in saucepan and heat enough to mix well. Pour over chicken. Cover and cook on LOW for 5 to 6 hours.

Serve chicken and sauce over noodles. Serves 4 to 6.

TIP: If chicken breasts are very large, cut in half lengthwise. This is great served with roasted garlic, oven-baked Italian toast.

Cheesy Mushroom Chicken Breasts

- **4 boneless, skinless chicken breast halves**
- **1 (10 ounce) can French onion soup** — **280 g**
- **2 teaspoons chicken seasoning** — **10 ml**
- **1 (4 ounce) jar sliced mushrooms, drained** — **115 g**
- **1 cup shredded mozzarella cheese** — **115 g**
- **Chopped green onions**

Brown each chicken breast in skillet and place in sprayed, oval slow cooker.

Pour onion soup over chicken and sprinkle black pepper and chicken seasoning over chicken breasts.

Place mushrooms and cheese over chicken breasts.

Cover and cook on LOW for 4 to 5 hours. To give this chicken a really nice touch when ready to serve, sprinkle some chopped green onions over each serving. Serves 4.

Southwestern Chicken Pot

- **6 boneless, skinless chicken breast halves**
- **1 teaspoon ground cumin** — **5 ml**
- **1 teaspoon chili powder** — **5 ml**
- **1 (10 ounce) can cream of chicken soup** — **280 g**
- **1 (10 ounce) can fiesta nacho cheese soup** — **280 g**
- **1 cup salsa** — **265 g**
- **Rice, cooked**
- **Flour tortillas**

Place chicken breasts sprinkled with cumin, chili powder and a little salt and pepper in sprayed, oval slow cooker.

Combine soups and salsa in saucepan. Heat just enough to mix and pour over chicken breasts. Cover and cook on LOW for 6 to 7 hours.

Serve over rice with warmed, flour tortillas spread with butter. Serves 4 to 6.

Orange-Seasoned Chicken

- **6 boneless, skinless chicken breast halves**
- **Canola oil**
- **1 (1 ounce) packet dry onion soup mix**   **30 g**
- **1 (6 ounce) can frozen orange juice concentrate, thawed**   **170 g**

Brown chicken breasts in little oil in skillet and place in sprayed, large slow cooker.

Combine onion soup mix, orange juice concentrate and ½ cup (125 ml) water in bowl and pour over chicken.

Cover and cook on LOW for 3 to 5 hours. Serves 4 to 6.

Sweet-and-Sour Chicken

- **6 boneless, skinless chicken breast halves**
- **2 carrots, sliced**
- **2 ribs celery, sliced**
- **1 onion, chopped**
- **⅓ cup Catalina dressing**   **75 ml**
- **⅓ cup packed brown sugar**   **75 g**
- **¼ cup soy sauce**   **60 ml**
- **1 (8 ounce) can pineapple chunks with liquid**   **225 g**
- **1 tablespoon cornstarch**   **15 ml**
- **1 green bell pepper, seeded, sliced**
- **1 red bell pepper, seeded, sliced**

Season chicken breasts and place in sprayed slow cooker. Place carrots, celery and onion around chicken.

In small bowl, mix dressing, brown sugar and soy sauce; pour over chicken. Cover and cook on LOW for 7 hours or until chicken juices are clear.

Pour pineapple juice into small bowl and mix with cornstarch. Pour into chicken to thicken gravy. Turn slow cooker to HIGH.

Add pineapple and bell peppers, cover and continue to cook for 30 to 45 minutes or until peppers are tender. Serves 6 to 8.

Sunday Chicken

- **4 large boneless, skinless chicken breast halves**
- **Chicken seasoning**
- **4 slices American cheese**
- **1 (10 ounce) can cream of celery soup**   **280 g**
- **½ cup sour cream**   **120 g**
- **1 (6 ounce) box chicken stuffing mix**   **170 g**
- **½ cup (1 stick) butter, melted**   **115 g**

Place chicken breasts in sprayed, oval slow cooker. Sprinkle each breast with chicken seasoning.

Place slice of cheese over each chicken breast. Combine celery soup and sour cream in bowl, mix well and spoon over chicken and cheese.

Sprinkle chicken stuffing mix over top of cheese. Drizzle melted butter over stuffing mix.

Cover and cook on LOW for 5 to 6 hours. Serves 4.

Cooking time on HIGH equals about half the cooking time on LOW.

Tasty Chicken-Rice and Veggies

- 4 boneless, skinless chicken breast halves
- 2 (10 ounce) jars sweet-and-sour sauce   2 (280 g)
- 1 (16 ounce) package frozen broccoli, cauliflower and
  carrots, thawed   455 g
- 1 (10 ounce) package frozen green peas, thawed   280 g
- 2 cups sliced celery   200 g
- 1 (6 ounce) package parmesan-butter rice mix   170 g
- ⅓ cup toasted, slivered almonds   55 g
- Rice, cooked

Cut chicken in 1-inch (2.5 cm) strips. Combine pieces, sweet-and-sour sauce and all vegetables in sprayed 6-quart (6 L) slow cooker.

Cover and cook on LOW for 4 to 6 hours.

When ready to serve, cook parmesan-butter rice according to package direction and fold in almonds. Serve chicken and vegetables over rice. Serves 4.

Honey-Baked Chicken

- 2 small fryer chickens, quartered
- ½ cup (1 stick) butter, melted   115 g
- ⅔ cup honey   230 g
- ¼ cup dijon-style mustard   60 g
- 1 teaspoon curry powder   5 ml

Place chicken pieces in sprayed, large slow cooker, skin-side up and sprinkle a little salt over chicken.

Combine butter, honey, mustard and curry powder in bowl and mix well. Pour butter-mustard mixture over chicken quarters.

Cover and cook on LOW for 6 to 8 hours. Baste chicken once during cooking. Serves 6 to 8.

Tangy Chicken

- 1 large fryer chicken, quartered
- 2 tablespoons butter   **30 g**
- ½ cup Heinz 57® sauce   **125 ml**
- 1 (15 ounce) can stewed tomatoes   **425 g**

Place chicken quarters in sprayed, large slow cooker.

Combine butter, 57 sauce and stewed tomatoes in saucepan. Heat just until butter melts and ingredients mix well. Pour over chicken.

Cover and cook on LOW for 5 to 6 hours. Serves 4 to 6.

Nutty Chicken Chop

- 2 - 3 cups cooked, chopped chicken   **280 - 420 g**
- 1 onion, chopped
- 1 bell pepper, seeded, chopped
- 4 ribs celery, chopped
- 1 cup nuts, toasted, chopped   **170 g**
- 1 cup mayonnaise   **225 g**
- 1 cup cubed Velveeta® cheese   **140 g**
- 1 cup shredded parmesan cheese   **100 g**
- 1 cup crushed potato chips   **55 g**

Mix chicken, onion, bell pepper, celery, nuts, mayonnaise and Velveeta® and place in slow cooker. Cover and cook on LOW for about 6 hours.

Before serving, sprinkle parmesan and potato chips over chicken. Serves 4.

Slow cookers do not brown meat. While it is an additional step in preparation, many cooks prefer the extra flavor and appearance created by browning meats before adding to the slow cooker. Browning also has the advantage of melting the fat which can then be drained from the meat.

Chicken with Orange Sauce

- **½ cup plus 2 tablespoons flour**   **75 g**
- **½ teaspoon ground nutmeg**   **2 ml**
- **½ teaspoon ground cinnamon**   **2 ml**
- **1 whole chicken, quartered**
- **2 large sweet potatoes, peeled, sliced**
- **1 (8 ounce) can pineapple chunks with juice**   **225 g**
- **1 (10 ounce) can cream of chicken soup**   **280 g**
- **⅔ cup orange juice**   **150 ml**
- **Rice, cooked**

Combine ½ cup (60 g) flour, nutmeg and cinnamon in bowl and coat chicken quarters.

Place sweet potatoes and pineapple in sprayed, large slow cooker. Arrange chicken on top. Combine chicken soup, orange juice and remaining flour in bowl and pour over chicken.

Cover and cook on LOW for 7 to 9 hours or on HIGH for 3 to 4 hours. Serve over rice. Serves 4 to 6.

Apple-Chicken Curry Kick

- ½ pound new (red) potatoes, halved   **225 g**
- 1 bell pepper, seeded, chopped
- 1 large onion, chopped
- 1 gala or Granny Smith apple, peeled, chopped
- ¼ cup golden raisins   **40 g**
- 1 tablespoon extra virgin olive oil   **15 ml**
- 2 teaspoons curry powder, divided   **10 ml**
- 6 boneless, skinless chicken breast halves
- 1 cup sour cream   **240 g**

Place red potatoes, bell pepper, onion, apple, raisins and olive oil in slow cooker. Sprinkle 1 teaspoon curry powder on top and stir well.

Season chicken with 1 teaspoon curry powder and salt and pepper. Place on top vegetables. Cover and cook on LOW for about 6 to 8 hours or until juices run clear.

Remove chicken and potatoes to oven-proof serving dish and keep warm in oven. Turn slow cooker to HIGH and mix sour cream with ingredients in cooker.

Cover and cook about 15 minutes or until hot. Pour over chicken and serve. Serves 4 to 6.

Tasty Chicken and Veggies

• 1 (2½ - 3 pound) whole chicken, quartered	1.2 - 1.3 kg
• 1 (16 ounce) package baby carrots	455 g
• 4 potatoes, peeled, sliced	
• 3 ribs celery, sliced	
• 1 onion, peeled, sliced	
• 1 cup Italian salad dressing	250 ml
• ⅔ cup chicken broth	150 ml

Place chicken quarters in sprayed 6-quart (6 L) slow cooker with carrots, potatoes, celery and onion.

Pour salad dressing and chicken broth over chicken and vegetables. Cover and cook on LOW for 6 to 8 hours. Serves 4 to 6.

"Baked" Chicken

• 1 cup white rice	200 g
• 2 (10 ounce) cans cream of chicken soup	2 (280 g)
• 1 (14 ounce) can chicken broth	395 g
• 1 (1 ounce) packet dry onion soup mix	30 g
• 1 chicken, quartered	

Place rice in sprayed 5 to 6-quart (5 to 6 L) oval slow cooker. Combine chicken soup, broth, 2 soup cans water and onion soup mix in saucepan and mix well. Heat just enough to mix ingredients.

Spoon half over rice and place 4 chicken quarters in slow cooker. Spoon remaining soup mixture over chicken.

Cover and cook on LOW for 5 to 6 hours. Serves 4 to 6.

It is important to trim fat from meat before putting in the slow cooker. Fat may create an unpleasant texture. Foods may also cook more quickly than desired if there is too much fat in the cooker.

Saffron Rice and Chicken

- 1 fryer-broiler chicken, quartered
- ½ teaspoon garlic powder   2 ml
- Canola oil
- 1 (14 ounce) can chicken broth   400 g
- 1 onion, chopped
- 1 green pepper, cored, seeded, quartered
- 1 yellow pepper, cored, seeded, quartered
- 1 (4 ounce) jar pimentos, drained   115 g
- ⅓ cup prepared bacon bits   20 g
- 2 tablespoons butter, melted   30 g
- 1 (5 ounce) package saffron yellow rice mix   145 g

Sprinkle chicken with garlic powder and a little salt and pepper.

Brown chicken quarters in little oil in skillet. Place chicken in sprayed, oval slow cooker and pour broth in slow cooker.

Combine, onion, bell peppers, pimentos and bacon bits in bowl and spoon over chicken quarters.

Cover and cook on LOW for 4 to 5 hours.

Carefully remove chicken quarters from cooker in bowl, stir in butter and rice mix and return chicken to cooker.

Cover and cook for additional 1 hour or until rice is tender. Serves 4 to 6.

Lemon Chicken

- **1 (2½ - 3 pound) chicken, quartered** — 1.2 - 1.3 kg
- **1 teaspoon dried oregano** — 5 ml
- **2 teaspoons minced garlic** — 10 ml
- **2 tablespoons butter** — 30 g
- **¼ cup lemon juice** — 60 ml

Season chicken quarters with salt, pepper and oregano and rub garlic on chicken.

Brown chicken quarters on all sides in butter in skillet and transfer to sprayed, oval slow cooker.

Add ⅓ cup (75 ml) water to skillet, scrape bottom and pour over chicken. Cover and cook on LOW for 6 to 8 hours.

At last hour of cooking, pour lemon juice over chicken, finish cooking. Serves 4 to 6.

Cooking time on HIGH equals about half the cooking time on LOW.

Chicken Coq au Vin

- **1 large fryer chicken, quartered, skinned**
- **Canola oil**
- **10 - 12 small white onions, peeled**
- **½ pound whole mushrooms**   **225 g**
- **1 teaspoon minced garlic**   **5 ml**
- **½ teaspoon dried thyme leaves**   **2 ml**
- **10 - 12 small new (red) potatoes with peels**
- **1 (10 ounce) can chicken broth**   **280 g**
- **1 cup burgundy wine**   **250 ml**
- **6 bacon slices, cooked, crumbled**

Brown chicken quarters in skillet on both sides and set aside. Place white onions, whole mushrooms, garlic and thyme in sprayed, oval slow cooker.

Add chicken quarters, potatoes, chicken broth and a little salt and pepper. Cover and cook on LOW for 8 to 10 hours or on HIGH for 3 to 4 hours.

During last hour, turn heat to HIGH, add wine and continue cooking. Sprinkle crumbled bacon over chicken before serving. Serves 4 to 6.

Chicken Marsala

- **4 boneless, skinless chicken breast halves**
- **1 teaspoon garlic powder**   **5 ml**
- **Dash of oregano**
- **Dash of basil**
- **¼ cup flour**   **30 g**
- **Canola oil**
- **½ cup (1 stick) butter**   **115 g**
- **1 (8 ounce) package cream cheese, softened**   **225 g**
- **1 cup marsala wine**   **250 ml**
- **2 (10 ounce) cans cream of mushroom soup**   **2 (280 g)**

Cut chicken in bite-size pieces. Season with garlic powder, oregano and basil, dredge in flour and brown in hot oil in skillet. Drain and place chicken in sprayed slow cooker.

In saucepan melt butter, cream cheese and add wine, ¾ cup water and soup and heat just until soup mixes. Pour over chicken and cook on LOW for 6 to 8 hours or until chicken juices are clear. Serves 4 to 6.

> *Chicken thighs are more flavorful and less likely to overcook than chicken breasts in slow cooker recipes.*

Chicken Cacciatore

- 2 onions, thinly sliced
- 1 (2½ - 3) pound fryer chicken, quartered — 1.2 - 1.3 kg
- 2 (6 ounce) cans tomato paste — 2 (170 g)
- 1 (4 ounce) can sliced mushrooms — 114 g
- 1½ teaspoons minced garlic — 7 ml
- ½ teaspoon dried basil — 2 ml
- 2 teaspoons oregano leaves — 10 ml
- ⅔ cup dry white wine — 150 ml

Place sliced onions in sprayed oval slow cooker. Place chicken quarters in slow cooker.

Combine tomato paste, mushrooms, garlic, basil, oregano and wine in bowl and pour over chicken quarters.

Cover and cook on LOW for 7 to 8 hours or on HIGH for 4 hours. Serves 4 to 6.

Pompei Chicken

- 2 pounds boneless, skinless chicken thighs — 910 g
- ¼ cup canola oil — 60 ml
- ½ cup flour — 60 g
- 1 (14 ounce) can stewed diced Italian-style tomatoes — 395 g
- ⅓ cup pitted Kalamata olives, quartered — 75 g
- ⅓ cup cabernet sauvignon — 75 ml
- 1 clove garlic, minced
- 1 teaspoon rosemary — 5 ml
- ½ teaspoon oregano — 2 ml
- ¼ teaspoon cayenne — 1 ml

Heat oil in skillet, dredge chicken pieces in flour and brown in skillet. Place drained chicken in slow cooker.

Combine all remaining ingredients in separate bowl and stir. Pour over chicken and cook on LOW for about 5 hours or until juices of chicken run clear. Serves 4 to 6.

Chicken Oscar

- **8 boneless, skinless chicken breast halves**
- **¼ cup flour** — **60 g**
- **1 (14 ounce) can Italian stewed tomatoes with juice** — **395 g**
- **1 tablespoon lemon juice** — **15 ml**
- **1 bell pepper, seeded, chopped**
- **1 onion, chopped**
- **1 carrot, chopped**

Season chicken with a little salt and pepper. Dredge pieces in flour and brown in skillet with hot oil. Place in sprayed slow cooker and pour tomatoes with juice on top. Cover and cook on LOW for 6 hours.

Add bell peppers, onion and carrot to slow cooker. Turn on HIGH and cook for additional 1 to 2 hours or until vegetables are tender and juices of chicken are clear. Serves 6 to 8.

Taco Chicken

- **3 cups cooked, chopped chicken** — **420 g**
- **1 (1 ounce) packet taco seasoning** — **30 g**
- **1 cup white rice** — **200 g**
- **2 cups chopped celery** — **200 g**
- **1 green bell pepper, seeded, chopped**
- **2 (15 ounce) cans Mexican stewed tomatoes** — **2 (425 g)**

Combine chicken, taco seasoning, rice, celery, bell pepper and stewed tomatoes in bowl and mix well.

Pour into sprayed 5-quart (5 L) slow cooker. Cover and cook on LOW for 4 to 5 hours. Serves 4 to 6.

TIP: This is a great recipe for leftover chicken.

Cilantro-Chicken Cutlets

- **6 boneless, skinless chicken breast halves**
- **1 teaspoon seasoned salt**   **5 ml**
- **1 teaspoon seasoned pepper**   **5 ml**
- **3 teaspoons cilantro, divided**   **15 ml**
- **1¼ teaspoons cumin, divided**   **7 ml**
- **¼ cup (½ stick) butter**   **55 g**
- **¼ cup flour**   **30 g**
- **2 cups milk**   **500 ml**
- **⅓ cup dry white wine**   **75 ml**
- **1 cup shredded Monterey Jack cheese**   **115 g**

Pound breasts to about ¼ inch thick, place chicken breasts in skillet with a little oil and brown on both sides. Season with pepper and place in sprayed slow cooker.

Melt butter in saucepan over low heat and stir in flour, cilantro, cumin, and a little salt and pepper. Add milk and heat just a little. Remove from heat and pour in wine.

Pour sauce over chicken. Cover and cook on LOW for 6 to 8 hours. Before serving, sprinkle cheese over top, cover and heat about 10 minutes. Serves 4 to 6.

Monterey Bake

• 6 (6 inch) corn tortillas	6 (15 cm)
• 3 cups leftover cubed chicken	420 g
• 1 (10 ounce) package frozen whole kernel corn	280 g
• 1 (15 ounce) can pinto beans with liquid	425 g
• 1 (16 ounce) hot jar salsa	455 g
• ¼ cup sour cream	60 g
• 1 tablespoon flour	15 ml
• 3 tablespoons snipped fresh cilantro	5 g
• 1 (8 ounce) package shredded 4-cheese blend	225 g

Preheat oven to 250° (120° C). Cut tortillas into 6 wedges. Place half of tortillas wedges in sprayed slow cooker. Place remaining wedges on baking pan, bake for about 10 minutes and set aside.

Layer chicken, corn and beans over tortillas in cooker. Combine salsa, sour cream, flour and cilantro in bowl and pour over corn and beans.

Cover and cook on LOW for 3 to 4 hours.

When ready to serve, place baked tortillas wedges and cheese on top of each serving. Serves 4 to 6.

Chicken with Stuffing and Broccoli

- 1 (10 ounce) can cream of chicken soup   280 g
- 2 stalks celery, sliced
- ½ cup (1 stick) butter, melted   115 g
- 3 cups cooked, cubed chicken   420 g
- 1 (16 ounce) package frozen broccoli, corn and red peppers   455 g
- 1 (8 ounce) box cornbread stuffing mix   225 g

Combine chicken soup, celery, butter, chicken, vegetables, stuffing mix and ⅓ cup (75 ml) water in large bowl.

Mix well and transfer to sprayed 5 or 6-quart (5 to 6 L) slow cooker. Cover and cook on LOW for 5 to 6 hours. Serves 4 to 6.

TIP: This is a great recipe for leftover chicken.

Chicken and Everything Good

- 2 (10 ounce) cans cream of chicken soup   2 (280 g)
- ⅓ cup (⅔ stick) butter, melted   75 g
- 3 cups cooked, cubed chicken   420 g
- 1 (16 ounce) package frozen broccoli, corn and red peppers   455 g
- 1 (10 ounce) package frozen green peas   280 g
- 1 (8 ounce) package cornbread stuffing mix   225 g

Combine soup, butter and ⅓ cup (75 ml) water in large bowl and mix well. Add chicken, vegetables and stuffing mix and stir well.

Spoon mixture into sprayed, large slow cooker. Cover and cook on LOW for 5 to 6 hours or on HIGH for 2 hours 30 minutes to 3 hours. Serves 4 to 6.

Because slow cooker recipes rely on blended flavors, they are usually just as good or even better when reheated in oven, microwave or on top of the stove.

Chicken Thighs Alfredo

- **1½ pounds boneless, skinless chicken thighs, cut into strips**   **680 g**
- **2 ribs celery, sliced diagonally**
- **1 red bell pepper, cored, seeded, julienned**
- **1 (16 ounce) jar alfredo sauce**   **455 g**
- **3 cups fresh broccoli florets**   **215 g**
- **1 (8 ounce) package fettuccini or linguine**   **225 g**
- **1 (4 ounce) package grated parmesan cheese**   **115 g**

Cut chicken into strips. Layer chicken, celery and bell pepper in sprayed 4 to 5-quart (4 to 5 L) slow cooker.

Pour alfredo sauce evenly over vegetables. Cover and cook on LOW for 5 to 6 hours.

About 30 minutes before serving, turn heat to HIGH and add broccoli florets to chicken-alfredo mixture. Cover and cook for additional 30 minutes.

Cook pasta according to package directions and drain. Just before serving pour pasta into cooker, mix and sprinkle parmesan cheese on top. Serves 4 to 6.

Chicken thighs are more flavorful and less likely to overcook than chicken breasts in slow cooker recipes.

Chicken Italiano

- **6 boneless, skinless chicken breast halves**
- **12 slices provolone cheese**
- **12 slices prosciutto**
- **½ cup flour**   **60 g**
- **½ cup shredded parmesan cheese**   **50 g**
- **Canola oil**
- **1 (10 ounce) can cream of mushroom soup**   **280 g**
- **¾ cup white wine**   **60 ml**

Lay chicken breasts out flat and cut in half. Place halves between wax paper and pound to ¼ to ½-inch thick. Place 1 slice provolone and 1 slice prosciutto over each half and roll up. Secure with toothpick.

Mix flour with a little salt and pepper and parmesan. Dredge chicken rolls through flour and fry in a little hot oil in skillet. Drain and place in slow cooker.

In saucepan, mix mushroom soup with wine and a little water if needed over medium heat to mix well. Pour over chicken rolls and cook on LOW for 6 hours or until chicken juices run clear. Serves 6 to 8.

Sweet and Spicy Chicken

- 2 pounds chicken thighs   910 g
- ¾ cup chili sauce   205 g
- ¾ cup packed brown sugar   165 g
- 1 (1 ounce) packet dry onion soup mix   30 g
- ¼ teaspoon cayenne pepper   1 ml
- Rice, cooked

Arrange chicken pieces in sprayed 5-quart (5 L) slow cooker.

Combine chili sauce, brown sugar, dry onion soup mix, cayenne pepper and ¼ cup (60 ml) water in bowl and spoon over chicken.

Cover and cook on LOW for 6 to 7 hours. Serve over rice. Serves 4 to 6.

Southern Chicken

- 1 cup half-and-half cream   310 g
- 1 tablespoon flour   15 ml
- 1 (1 ounce) packet chicken gravy mix   30 g
- 1 pound boneless, skinless chicken thighs   455 g
- 1 (16 ounce) package frozen stew vegetables, thawed   455 g
- 1 (4 ounce) jar sliced mushrooms, drained   115 g
- 1 (10 ounce) package frozen green peas, thawed   280 g
- 1½ cups biscuit mix   180 g
- 1 bunch fresh green onions, chopped
- ½ cup milk   125 ml

Combine cream, flour, gravy mix and 1 cup (250 ml) water in bowl, stir until smooth and pour in sprayed, large slow cooker.

Cut chicken into 1-inch (2.5 cm) pieces and stir in vegetables and mushrooms.

Cover and cook on LOW for 4 to 6 hours or until chicken is tender and sauce thickens. Stir in peas.

Combine biscuit mix, onions and milk in bowl and mix well. Drop tablespoonfuls of dough onto chicken mixture. Turn slow cooker to HIGH, cover and cook for additional 50 to 60 minutes. Serves 4 to 6.

Italian Chicken

- 1 small head cabbage
- 1 onion
- 1 (4 ounce) jar sliced mushrooms, drained   115 g
- 1 medium zucchini, sliced
- 1 red bell pepper, cored, seeded, julienned
- 1 teaspoon Italian seasoning   5 ml
- 1½ pounds boneless, skinless chicken thighs   680 g
- 1 teaspoon minced garlic   5 ml
- 2 (15 ounce) cans Italian stewed tomatoes   2 (425 g)
- Parmesan cheese

Cut cabbage into wedges, slice onions and separate into rings. Make layers of cabbage, onion, mushrooms, zucchini and bell pepper in sprayed 6-quart (6 L) slow cooker.

Sprinkle Italian seasoning over vegetables. Place chicken thighs on top of vegetables.

Mix garlic with tomatoes in bowl and pour over chicken. Cover and cook on LOW for 4 to 6 hours. When serving, sprinkle a little parmesan cheese over each serving. Serves 4 to 6.

Creamy Angel Hair Pasta Chicken

• 1 (10 ounce) can cream of mushroom soup	280 g
• 1 (8 ounce) package cream cheese, softened	225 g
• ½ cup dry white wine	125 ml
• ⅓ cup Italian vinaigrette dressing	75 ml
• 2½ - 3 pounds boneless, skinless chicken thighs	1.1 - 1.4 kg
• ½ pound angel hair pasta	225 g
• Shredded parmesan cheese	

Heat mushroom soup with 1 soup can water in saucepan over medium heat. Add cream cheese, wine and dressing and blend well.

Cut thighs into bite-size pieces and place in sprayed slow cooker. Pour soup mixture over chicken. Cover and cook on LOW for 6 to 7 hours or until juices of chicken are clear.

Cook pasta according to package directions. Place in slow cooker and stir chicken and sauce on pasta.

Cover and cook about 15 to 20 minutes to heat through. Serve with a little shredded parmesan on top. Serves 8 to 10.

Asparagus-Cheese Chicken

• 8 - 10 boneless, skinless chicken thighs	
• 2 tablespoons butter	30 g
• 1 (10 ounce) can cream of celery soup	280 g
• 1 (10 ounce) can cheddar cheese soup	280 g
• ⅓ cup milk	75 ml
• 1 (16 ounce) package frozen asparagus cuts	455 g

Place chicken thighs in sprayed 5-quart (5 L) slow cooker. Combine butter, celery soup, cheddar cheese soup and milk in saucepan.

Heat just enough for butter to melt and mix well. Pour over chicken thighs. Cover and cook on LOW for 5 to 6 hours.

Remove cover and place asparagus cuts over chicken and cook for additional 1 hour. Serves 4 to 6.

Arroz con Pollo

Rice with Chicken

- **3 pounds chicken thighs**
- **2 (15 ounce) cans Italian stewed tomatoes** — 2 (425 g)
- **1 (16 ounce) package frozen green peas, thawed** — 455 g
- **2 cups long grain rice** — 370 g
- **1 (.28 ounce) packet yellow rice seasoning mix** — 10 g
- **2 (14 ounce) cans chicken broth** — 2 (395 g)
- **1 heaping teaspoon minced garlic** — 5 ml
- **1 teaspoon dried oregano** — 5 ml

Combine all ingredients plus ¾ cup (175 ml) water in sprayed, large slow cooker and stir well.

Cover and cook on LOW for 7 to 8 hours or on HIGH for 3 hours 30 minutes to 4 hours. Serves 6 to 8.

Cheesy Chicken and Noodles

- **1 (8 ounce) package wide noodles** — 225 g
- **1 (10 ounce) can cream of chicken soup** — 280 g
- **4 cups cooked, chopped chicken breasts** — 560 g
- **1 (15 ounce) package ricotta cheese, softened, cubed** — 425 g
- **1 (8 ounce) package shredded mozzarella cheese** — 225 g
- **1 (16 ounce) package frozen chopped onions and bell peppers** — 455 g
- **2 ribs celery, sliced**
- **1 (10 ounce) can chicken broth** — 280 g
- **1 teaspoon white pepper** — 1 ml

Cook noodles according to package directions and drain. Place noodles, soup, chicken, ricotta cheese, mozzarella cheese, onions and bell peppers, celery and broth in sprayed slow cooker; stir until ingredients blend well.

Sprinkle white pepper over top of ingredients and cook on LOW for 7 to 9 hours or on HIGH for 3 hours 30 minutes. Serves 6.

Stupendous Rice and Chicken

- **2 (10 ounce) cans cream of chicken soup**   **2 (280 g)**
- **2 (4 ounce) boxes long grain-wild rice mix**   **2 (115 g)**
- **1 red bell pepper, seeded, cut into strips**
- **1 green bell pepper, seeded, cut into strips**
- **1 (4 ounce) can sliced mushrooms**   **115 g**
- **4 - 5 boneless, skinless chicken breast halves**

Combine chicken soup, rice, seasoning packets and 2 cups (500 ml) water in large bowl.

Pour half mixture into sprayed 4 to 5 (4 to 5 L) slow cooker (must be large slow cooker because rice will expand during cooking).

Layer bell pepper strips, mushrooms, and chicken breasts on top and pour remaining soup-rice mixture over chicken.

Cover and cook on LOW for 6 to 7 hours or on HIGH for 3 to 4 hours. Do not cook any longer than above times because rice will become mushy if over cooked. Serves 4 to 5.

Tangy Chicken Legs

- **12 - 15 chicken legs**
- **⅓ cup soy sauce**   **75 ml**
- **⅔ cup packed brown sugar**   **150 g**
- **Scant ⅛ teaspoon ground ginger**   **.5 ml**

Place chicken legs in sprayed 5-quart (5 L) slow cooker. Combine soy sauce, brown sugar, ¼ cup (60 ml) water and ginger in bowl and spoon over chicken legs.

Cover and cook on LOW for 4 to 5 hours. Serves 6 to 8.

Add ingredients in the order given for all slow cooker recipes unless stated otherwise in the directions.

Three Hour Chicken

- 1 (10 ounce) can cream of chicken soup   280 g
- 1 (4 ounce) can sliced mushrooms   115 g
- 1 small onion, finely chopped
- 1 teaspoon Italian seasoning   5 ml
- 1½ pounds boneless, skinless chicken breasts, cut into strips   680 g
- Rice, cooked

Combine soup, mushrooms, onion and seasonings in sprayed slow cooker. Add chicken strips.

Cover and cook on LOW for 2 hours 30 minutes to 3 hours. Serve over rice. Serves 4.

Yes to This Chicken

- 5 - 6 boneless, skinless chicken breast halves
- 1 (8 ounce) bottle Italian-style salad dressing   235 ml
- 1 (10 ounce) can chicken broth   280 g
- 1 (11 ounce) can Mexicorn®, drained   310 g
- 1 (8 ounce) package shredded Velveeta® cheese   225 g
- ¾ teaspoon dried basil   4 ml
- 1 (12 ounce) package pasta   340 g

Place chicken breasts in sprayed oval slow cooker. Pour salad dressing over chicken; cover and cook on LOW for 6 to 8 hours.

Drain juices from slow cooker and stir in broth, corn, cheese, basil and a little salt and pepper. Combine and cook on LOW for additional 1 hour.

Cook your favorite pasta, drain and place on serving platter. Place chicken over pasta and spoon mixture over chicken breasts. Serves 5 to 6.

Maple-Plum Glazed Turkey Breast

- 1 cup red plum jam   320 g
- 1 cup maple syrup   250 ml
- 1 teaspoon dry mustard   5 ml
- ¼ cup lemon juice   60 ml
- 1 (3 - 5 pound) boneless turkey breast   1.3 - 2.2 kg

Combine jam, syrup, mustard and lemon juice in saucepan. Bring to a boil, turn heat down and simmer for about 20 minutes or until slightly thick. Set aside 1 cup (250 ml).

Place turkey breast in sprayed slow cooker and pour remaining glaze over turkey. Cover and cook on LOW for 5 to 7 hours.

When ready to serve, slice turkey and serve with heated set aside glaze. Serves 6 to 8.

Turkey Bake

- 1½ pounds turkey tenderloins   680 g
- 1 (6 ounce) package Oriental rice and vermicelli   170 g
- 1 (10 ounce) package frozen green peas, thawed   280 g
- 1 cup sliced celery   100 g
- ¼ cup (½ stick) butter, melted   60 g
- 1 (14 ounce) can chicken broth   395 g
- 1½ cups fresh broccoli florets   105 g

Cut tenderloins into strips. Saute turkey strips in non-stick skillet until it is no longer pink.

Combine turkey strips, rice-vermicelli mix plus seasoning packet, peas, celery, butter, chicken broth and 1 cup (250 ml) water in sprayed, large slow cooker and mix well.

Cover and cook on LOW for 4 to 5 hours. Turn heat to HIGH setting, add broccoli and cook for additional 20 minutes. Serves 4 to 6.

Easy Turkey Main Dish

- 1 turkey breast
- 1 (15 ounce) can whole berry cranberry sauce   425 g
- 2 ribs celery, diced
- 2 green onions with tops, diced
- ½ cup orange juice   125 ml
- 1 teaspoon lemon juice   5 ml
- 1 packet dry onion soup mix   30 g

Place turkey in sprayed slow cooker. In bowl mix all remaining ingredients and pour over turkey. Cover and cook on LOW for about 8 hours. Serves 4 to 6.

Cranberry Harvest Turkey

- 1 (2 - 3 pound) boneless, skinless, seasoned, precooked
  turkey breast half   910 g - 1.4 kg
- ½ cup orange marmalade   160 g
- 1 (15 ounce) can whole cranberry sauce   425g

Place turkey breast in sprayed slow cooker and pour marmalade and cranberries over turkey. Cook on LOW for about 4 to 6 hours or until heated through. Serves 4 to 6.

Turkey Cassoulet

- **2 cups cooked, cubed turkey**   **280 g**
- **1 (8 ounce) package smoked turkey sausage**   **225 g**
- **3 carrots, sliced**
- **1 onion, halved, sliced**
- **1 (15 ounce) can navy bean**   **425 g**
- **1 (15 ounce) can white lima beans**   **425 g**
- **1 (8 ounce) can tomato sauce**   **225 g**
- **1 teaspoon dried thyme**   **5 ml**
- **¼ teaspoon ground allspice**   **1 ml**

Cut turkey sausage in ½-inch (1.2 cm) pieces. Combine all ingredients in sprayed slow cooker.

Cover and cook on LOW for 4 to 5 hours. Serves 4.

TIP: This is a great recipe for leftover turkey

Turkey Loaf

- **2 pounds ground turkey**   **910 g**
- **1 onion, very finely chopped**
- **½ red bell pepper, very finely chopped**
- **2 teaspoons minced garlic**   **10 ml**
- **½ cup chili sauce**   **135 g**
- **2 large eggs, beaten**
- **¾ cup Italian seasoned breadcrumbs**   **175 ml**

Make foil handles by cutting 3 (3 x 18-inch/8 x 45 cm) strips of heavy foil. Place in bottom of slow cooker in crisscross strips (resembles spokes on wheel) up and over sides.

Combine all ingredients plus 1 teaspoon (5 ml) salt and ½ teaspoon (2 ml) pepper in large bowl and mix well.

Shape into round loaf and place on top of the foil. Fold extended strips over food. When finished cooking, lift food out by handles.

Cover and cook on LOW for 5 to 6 hours. Serves 4 to 6.

*Recipes in this cookbook may be cooked in 3 to 6-quart slow cookers.
You may need to adjust the quantity of ingredients for a smaller cooker.*

Turkey Spaghetti

• 2 pounds ground turkey	910 g
• 2 (10 ounce) cans tomato bisque soup	2 (280 g)
• 1 (14 ounce) can chicken broth	395 g
• 2 (7 ounce) boxes ready-cut spaghetti, cooked, drained	2 (200 g)
• 1 (15 ounce) can whole kernel corn, drained	425 g
• 1 (4 ounce) can sliced mushrooms, drained	115 g
• ¼ cup ketchup	70 g

Cook ground turkey in non-stick skillet and season with a little salt and pepper. Place cooked turkey in sprayed 5 to 6-quart (5 to 6 L) slow cooker.

Add in soup, broth. spaghetti, corn, mushrooms and ketchup and stir to blend. Cover and cook on LOW for 5 to 7 hours or on HIGH for 3 hours. Serves 4 to 6.

Colorful Rice and Turkey

• 1 (10 ounce) can cream of mushroom soup	280 g
• 1 (10 ounce) can cream of chicken soup	280 g
• 2 cups white rice	200 g
• 3 ribs celery, sliced diagonally	
• 1 (16 ounce) package frozen Oriental vegetable mix	455 g
• 3 cups cooked, cubed turkey	420 g
• 1 teaspoon poultry seasoning	5 ml
• 2 (14 ounce) cans chicken broth	2 (395 g)

Pour mushroom soup and chicken soup in saucepan and add 1 soup can water. Heat just enough to mix well and pour into sprayed 5 to 6-quart (5 to 6 L) slow cooker.

Add remaining ingredients and mix. Cover and cook on LOW for 5 to 6 hours. Serves 4 to 6.

Sausage and Rice

- 1 pound turkey sausage   455 g
- 1 (6 ounce) box flavored rice mix   170 g
- 2 (14 ounce) cans chicken broth   2 (395 g)
- 2 cups sliced celery   200 g
- 1 red bell pepper, cored, seeded, julienned
- 1 (15 ounce) can cut green beans, drained   425 g
- ⅓ cup slivered almonds, toasted   55 g

Break up turkey sausage and brown in skillet. Place in sprayed 4 to 5-quart (4 to 5 L) slow cooker.

Add rice, 1 cup (250 ml) water, chicken broth, celery, bell pepper and green beans and stir to mix. Cover and cook on LOW for 3 to 4 hours.

When ready to serve, sprinkle almonds over top. Serves 4.

Beef
Main
Dishes

Smothered Mushroom Beef Tips

- 2 (10 ounce) cans golden mushroom soup   2 (280 g)
- 1 (14 ounce) can beef broth   395 g
- 1 tablespoon beef seasoning   15 ml
- 2 (4 ounce) cans sliced mushrooms, drained   2 (115 g)
- 2 pounds round steak, cut in slices   910 g
- Noodles
- 1 (8 ounce) carton sour cream   225 g

Combine soups, beef broth, beef seasoning and sliced mushrooms in bowl. Place in sprayed slow cooker and stir to blend.

Add slices of beef and stir well. Cover and cook on LOW for 4 to 5 hours. When ready to serve, cook noodles, drain, add salt and a little butter.

Stir sour cream into sauce in slow cooker. Spoon sauce and beef over noodles. Serves 4 to 6.

Salsa-Mushroom Steak

This recipe makes a great sauce for mashed potatoes.

- 1½ pounds lean round steak   680 g
- 1 onion, halved, sliced
- 2 (10 ounce) cans golden mushroom soup   2 (280 g)
- 1½ cups hot, thick-and-chunky salsa   360 ml

Trim fat from steak and cut into serving-size pieces. Sprinkle with 1 teaspoon (5 ml) pepper and place in sprayed 5 to 6-quart (5 to 6 L) slow cooker.

Place onion slices over steak. Combine mushroom soup and salsa in bowl and mix well. Spoon over steak and onions.

Cover and cook on LOW for 7 to 8 hours. Serves 4 to 6.

Cooking time on HIGH equals about half the cooking time on LOW.

Pepper Steak over Noodles

- 1½ pounds round steak   680 g
- Canola oil
- ¼ cup soy sauce   60 ml
- 1 onion, sliced
- 1 teaspoon minced garlic   5 ml
- 1 teaspoon sugar   5 ml
- ¼ teaspoon ground ginger   1 ml
- 1 (15 ounce) can stewed tomatoes   425 g
- 2 green bell peppers, cored, seeded, julienned
- 1 teaspoon beef bouillon granules   5 ml
- 1 tablespoon cornstarch   15 ml
- Rice or noodles, cooked

Slice beef in strips, brown in skillet with a little oil and place in sprayed, oval slow cooker. Combine soy sauce, onion, garlic, sugar and ginger in bowl and pour over beef.

Cover and cook on LOW for 5 to 6 hours. Add tomatoes, bell peppers and bouillon and cook for additional 1 hour.

Combine cornstarch and ¼ cup water (60 ml) in cup and stir into cooker. Continue cooking until liquid thickens. Serve over rice or noodles. Serves 4 to 6.

Easy Swiss Steak

- 1 - 1½ pounds boneless, round steak .... 455 - 680 g
- ½ teaspoon seasoned salt .... 2 ml
- ½ teaspoon seasoned pepper .... 2 ml
- 8 - 10 medium new (red) potatoes with peels, halved
- 1 cup baby carrots .... 135 g
- 1 onion, sliced
- 1 (15 ounce) can stewed tomatoes .... 425 g
- 1 (12 ounce) jar beef gravy .... 340 g

Cut steak in 6 to 8 serving-size pieces, season with seasoned salt and pepper and brown in non-stick skillet.

Layer steak pieces, potatoes, carrots and onion in sprayed slow cooker. Combine tomatoes and beef gravy in bowl and spoon over vegetables.

Cover and cook on LOW for 7 to 8 hours. Serves 4 to 6.

Spicy Bratwurst Steak

- 1½ pounds boneless, beef round steak .... 680 g
- 4 ounces spicy bratwurst .... 115 g
- 2 small onions
- 2 tablespoons quick-cooking tapioca .... 35 g
- 1 teaspoon dried thyme .... 5 ml
- 2 (15 ounce) cans Mexican stewed tomatoes .... 2 (425 g)
- Noodles, cooked

Trim fat from steak and cut into 4 serving-size pieces. Brown steak and bratwurst in skillet. Drain and place in sprayed 4 to 5-quart (4 to 5 L) slow cooker.

Slice onions and separate into rings. Cover meat with onions and sprinkle with tapioca, thyme, a little salt and pepper.

Pour stewed tomatoes over onion and seasonings. Cover and cook on LOW for 5 to 8 hours. Serve over noodles. Serves 4 to 6.

Beef-Mushroom Stroganoff

• **2 pounds beef round steak**	**910 g**
• **¾ cup flour, divided**	**90 g**
• **½ teaspoon mustard**	**2 ml**
• **2 onions, thinly sliced**	
• **½ pound fresh mushrooms, sliced**	**225 g**
• **1 (10 ounce) can beef broth**	**280 g**
• **¼ cup dry white wine or cooking wine**	**60 ml**
• **1 (8 ounce) carton sour cream**	**225 g**

Trim excess fat from steak and cut into 3-inch (8 cm) strips about ½ inch (1.2 cm) wide.

Combine ½ cup (60 ml) flour, mustard and a little salt and pepper in bowl and toss with steak strips.

Place strips in sprayed, oval slow cooker. Cover with onions and mushrooms. Add beef broth and wine. Cover and cook on LOW for 8 to 10 hours.

Just before serving, combine sour cream and ¼ cup (60 ml) flour in bowl. Stir into cooker and cook for additional 10 to 15 minutes or until stroganoff thickens slightly. Serves 4 to 6.

Teriyaki Steak

- 1½ - 2 pounds flank steak   680 - 910 g
- 1 (15 ounce) can sliced pineapple with juice   425 g
- 1 tablespoon marinade for chicken   15 ml
- ⅓ cup packed brown sugar   75 g
- 3 tablespoons soy sauce   45 ml
- ½ teaspoon ground ginger   2 ml
- 1 (14 ounce) can chicken broth   400 g
- 1 cup long grain rice   200 g

Roll flank steak, tie in place and cut into 7 to 8 individual steaks.

Combine ½ cup (125 ml) pineapple juice, marinade for chicken, brown sugar, soy sauce and ginger in bowl large enough for marinade to cover individual steaks.

Add steak rolls and marinate for 1 hour in sauce. Pour chicken broth into sprayed slow cooker.

Add rice and ¾ cup (175 ml) water. Place steaks over rice and broth. Cover and cook on LOW for 8 to 10 hours. Serves 4 to 6.

Smothered Steak

- 1 (2 pound) round steak   910 g
- 1 onion, chopped
- 1 (1 ounce) packet dry onion soup mix   30 g
- 1 (10 ounce) can cream of mushroom soup   280 g
- 1 (12 ounce) carton fresh button mushrooms, stemmed, sliced   340 g

Brown round steak in a little oil in large skillet. Place in sprayed slow cooker. Sprinkle onion soup mix over steak.

Mix mushroom soup and 1 soup can water in saucepan and heat just enough to mix. Pour over steak and pour mushrooms on top.

Cover and cook on LOW for 6 to 8 hours or until steak falls apart. Serves 4 to 6.

Mushroom-Round Steak

- **1½ - 2 pounds round steak**   **680 - 910 g**
- **1 (1 ounce) packet onion soup mix**   **30 g**
- **½ cup dry red wine**   **125 ml**
- **1 (8 ounce) carton fresh mushrooms, sliced**   **225 g**
- **1 (10 ounce) can French onion soup**   **280 g**

Cut round steak in serving-size pieces and place in sprayed, oval slow cooker.

Combine soup mix, red wine, mushrooms, French onion soup and ½ cup (125 ml) water in bowl, spoon over steak pieces.

Cover and cook on LOW for 7 to 8 hours. Serves 4 to 6.

Steak in Red Wine Sauce

- **1 pound round steak, cubed**   **455 g**
- **2 cups fresh mushroom halves**   **145 g**
- **1 (15 ounce) can Italian stewed tomatoes**   **425 g**
- **1 (10 ounce) can beef broth**   **280 g**
- **½ cup red wine**   **125 ml**
- **2 teaspoons Italian seasoning**   **10 ml**
- **3 tablespoons quick-cooking tapioca**   **50 g**
- **Linguine, cooked**

Place beef in sprayed slow cooker. Combine mushrooms, tomatoes, beef broth, wine, Italian seasoning, tapioca and a little salt and pepper in bowl. Pour over steak.

Cover and cook on LOW for 8 to 10 hours. Serve over linguine. Serves 4.

Do not assemble food in the ceramic insert the previous night and refrigerate. It will take additional time to cook. It is important that food reach a temperature of 165° (75° C) while cooking to ensure food safety.

Seasoned Round Steak

- **1 - 1½ pounds round steak**   **455 - 680 g**
- **1 onion**
- **2 cups fresh sliced mushrooms**   **145 g**
- **1 (10 ounce) can French onion soup**   **280 g**
- **1 (6 ounce) package herb stuffing mix**   **170 g**
- **½ cup (1 stick) butter, melted**   **115 g**

Cut beef into 5 to 6 serving-size pieces. Slice onion and separate into rings. Place steak pieces in sprayed, oval slow cooker and top with onions and mushrooms.

Pour soup over ingredients in cooker. Cover and cook on LOW for 7 to 9 hours.

Just before serving, combine stuffing mix, butter and ½ cup (125 ml) liquid from cooker and toss to mix.

Place stuffing mixture on top of steak and increase heat to HIGH. Cover and cook for additional 15 minutes or until stuffing is fluffy. Serves 4 to 6.

Beef Roulades

- 1½ pounds beef flank steak   680 g
- 5 slices bacon
- ¾ cup finely chopped onion   120 g
- 1 (4 ounce) can mushrooms pieces   115 g
- 1 tablespoon Worcestershire sauce   15 ml
- ⅓ cup Italian-seasoned breadcrumbs   40 g
- 1 (12 ounce) jar beef gravy   340 g
- Mashed potatoes

Cut steak into 4 to 6 serving-size pieces. Cut bacon into small pieces and combine with onion, mushrooms, Worcestershire and breadcrumbs in bowl. Place about ½ cup (125 ml) onion mixture on each piece of steak.

Roll meat and secure ends with toothpicks. Dry beef rolls with paper towels. In skillet, brown steak rolls and transfer to sprayed slow cooker.

Pour gravy evenly over steaks to thoroughly moisten. Cover and cook on LOW for 7 to 9 hours. Serves 4 to 6.

TIP: *This is really good served with mashed potatoes. Try instant mashed potatoes as a time-saver.*

Cooking time on HIGH equals about half the cooking time on LOW.

197

Beef Tips over Noodles

- ½ cup plus 3 tablespoons flour, divided   80 g
- 3 pounds beef tips   1.3 kg
- 1 (8 ounce) carton fresh mushrooms, sliced   225 g
- 1 bunch fresh green onions, chopped
- 1 small red bell pepper, seeded, chopped
- ¼ cup ketchup   70 g
- 1 (14 ounce) can beef broth   395 g
- 1 tablespoon Worcestershire sauce   15 ml
- Noodles, cooked

Coat beef tips with ½ cup (60 g) flour in bowl and transfer to sprayed slow cooker.

Add mushrooms, onion, bell pepper, ketchup, broth, Worcestershire sauce and a little salt and pepper.

Cover and cook on LOW for 8 to 9 hours. About 1 hour before serving, turn heat to HIGH.

Combine remaining flour with ¼ cup (60 ml) water in small bowl, stir into cooker and cook until liquid thickens.

Serve over noodles. Serves 6 to 8.

Beef Tips over Pasta

- 2 - 2½ pounds lean, beef stew meat   910 g
- 2 cups frozen, small whole onions, thawed   320 g
- 1 green bell pepper, seeded
- 1 (6 ounce) jar pitted Greek olives or ripe olives   170 g
- ½ cup sun-dried tomatoes in oil, drained, chopped   30 g
- 1 (28 ounce) jar marinara sauce   795 g
- 1 (8 ounce) package pasta twirls, cooked   225 g

Place beef and onions in sprayed 4 to 5-quart (4 to 5 L) slow cooker. Cut bell pepper in 1-inch (2.5 cm) cubes and add to slow cooker.

Add olives and tomatoes and pour marinara sauce over top. Cover and cook on LOW for 8 to 10 hours.

Serve over pasta twirls. Serves 4 to 6.

Barbecued Beef

- 1 (2 pound) boneless chuck roast   910 g
- ½ cup flour   60 g
- Canola oil
- 1 onion, sliced
- ½ cup chili sauce   135 g
- ¾ cup packed brown sugar   165 g
- ¼ cup red wine vinegar   60 ml
- 1 tablespoon Worcestershire sauce   15 ml
- 1 (16 ounce) package baby carrots   455 g

Cut beef into 1-inch (2.5 cm) cubes and dredge in flour and a little salt and pepper. Brown beef in a little oil in skillet and place in sprayed slow cooker.

Add remaining ingredients, except carrots, and 1 cup (250 ml) water. Cover and cook on LOW for 7 to 8 hours.

Add carrots and cook for additional 1 hour 30 minutes. Serves 4 to 6.

Sunday Pot Roast

- **1 (2 pound) chuck roast**   **910 g**
- **4 - 5 medium potatoes, peeled, quartered**
- **4 large carrots, quartered**
- **1 onion, quartered**
- **1 (14 ounce) can beef broth, divided**   **395 g**
- **2 tablespoons cornstarch**   **15 g**

Trim fat from pieces of roast. Cut roast into 2 equal pieces. Brown pieces of roast in skillet. (Coat pieces with flour, salt and pepper if you'd like a little "breading" on the outside.)

Place potatoes, carrots and onion in sprayed 4 to 5-quart (4 to 5 L) slow cooker and mix well. Place browned beef over vegetables.

Pour 1½ cups (375 ml) broth over beef and vegetables. Save remaining broth and refrigerate. Cover and cook on LOW for 8 to 9 hours.

About 5 minutes before serving, remove beef and vegetables with slotted spoon and place on serving platter. Cover to keep warm. Pour liquid from slow cooker into medium saucepan.

Blend remaining ½ cup (125 ml) broth and cornstarch in bowl until smooth and add to liquid in saucepan. Boil for 1 minute and stir constantly to thicken gravy.

Serve gravy with roast and veggies and season with a little salt and pepper, if desired. Serves 4 to 6.

Old-Time Pot Roast

- 1 (2 - 2½) pound boneless rump roast   910 g
- 5 medium potatoes, peeled, quartered
- 1 (16 ounce) package peeled baby carrots   455 g
- 2 medium onions, quartered
- 1 (10 ounce) can golden mushroom soup   280 g
- ½ teaspoon dried basil   2 ml
- ½ teaspoon seasoned salt   2 ml

Brown roast on all sides in large, non-stick skillet. Place potatoes, carrots and onions in sprayed 4 to 5-quart (4 to 5 L) slow cooker.

Place browned roast on top of vegetables. Combine soup, basil and seasoned salt in bowl and pour mixture over meat and vegetables.

Cover and cook on LOW for 9 to 11 hours. Serves 4 to 6.

TIP: To serve, transfer roast and vegetables to serving plate. Stir juices remaining in slow cooker and spoon over roast and vegetables.

Potato-Roast Mix

- 3 cups cooked, cubed beef roast   420 g
- 1 (28 ounce) package frozen hash browns with onions and peppers, thawed   795 g
- Canola oil
- 1 onion, chopped
- 1 (16 ounce) jar salsa   455 g
- 1 tablespoon beef seasoning   15 ml
- 1 cup shredded cheddar-Jack cheese   116 g

Place beef in sprayed, large slow cooker. Brown potatoes in little oil in large skillet. Stir in salsa and beef seasoning and transfer to slow cooker.

Cover and cook on HIGH for 4 to 5 hours. When ready to serve, sprinkle cheese over top. Serves 4.

Herb-Crusted Beef Roast

- 1 (2 - 3 pound) beef rump roast   910 g - 1.3 kg
- ¼ cup chopped fresh parsley   15 g
- ¼ cup chopped fresh oregano leaves   15 g
- ½ teaspoon dried rosemary leaves   2 ml
- 1 teaspoon minced garlic   5 ml
- 1 tablespoon oil   15 ml
- 6 slices thick-cut bacon

Rub roast with a little salt and pepper. Combine parsley, oregano, rosemary, garlic and oil in small bowl and press mixture on top and sides of roast.

Place roast in sprayed slow cooker. Place bacon over top of beef and tuck ends under bottom. Cover and cook on LOW for 6 to 8 hours. Serves 4 to 6.

Cola Roast

- 1 (4 pound) chuck roast   1.8 kg
- 1 (12 ounce) bottle chili sauce   340 g
- 1 onion, chopped
- 1 (12 ounce) can cola   340 g
- 1 tablespoon Worcestershire sauce   15 ml

Score roast in several places and fill each slit with a little salt and pepper. Sear roast in skillet on all sides. Place in sprayed 5-quart (5 L) slow cooker.

Combine chili sauce, onion, cola and Worcestershire in bowl and mix well. Pour over roast. Cover and cook on LOW for 8 to 9 hours. Serves 6 to 8.

Condensation forms on the inside of the lid and forms a seal while cooking with a slow cooker. This is why it is important not to lift the lid during the cooking period unless the recipe gives instructions to do so. It is also why the lids are usually glass – just so we can take a peek without lifting the lid!

Soda Pop Roast

- **1 (3 - 3½ pound) chuck roast**   **1.4 - 1.6 kg**
- **1 (1 ounce) packet dry onion soup mix**   **30 g**
- **2 (12 ounce) cans cola soda**   **2 (355 ml)**

Brown roast on all sides in skillet with a little oil. Place roast in sprayed slow cooker. Pour onion soup mix and sodas over roast. Cover and cook on LOW for 6 to 8 hours. Serves 6 to 8.

Classic Beef Roast

- **1 (3 - 4 pound) beef chuck roast**   **1.3 - 1.8 kg**
- **1 (1 ounce) packet onion soup mix**   **30 g**
- **2 (10 ounce) cans golden onion soup**   **2 (280 g)**
- **3 - 4 medium potatoes, quartered**

Place roast in sprayed, large slow cooker. Sprinkle soup mix on roast and spoon on soup. Place potatoes around roast.

Cover and cook on LOW for 7 to 8 hours or on HIGH for 4 hours. Serves 6 to 8.

Mushroom Beef

- 1 (10 ounce) can beefy mushroom soup   280 g
- 1 (10 ounce) can golden mushroom soup   280 g
- 1 (10 ounce) can French onion soup   280 g
- ⅓ cup seasoned breadcrumbs   40 g
- 2½ pounds lean beef stew meat   1.2 kg
- Noodles, cooked

Combine soups, ½ teaspoon (2 ml) pepper, breadcrumbs and ¾ cup (175 ml) water in sprayed 6-quart (6 L) slow cooker. Stir in beef cubes and mix well.

Cover and cook on LOW for 8 to 9 hours. Serve over noodles. Serves 6 to 8.

Beef Roast and Gravy

- 1 (4 pound) boneless rump roast   1.8 kg
- ½ cup flour, divided   60 g
- 1 (1 ounce) packet brown gravy mix   30 g
- 1 (1 ounce) packet beefy onion soup mix   30 g

Cut roast in half (if needed to fit into cooker). Place roast in sprayed 5 to 6-quart (5 to 6 L) slow cooker and rub half of flour over roast.

Combine remaining flour, gravy mix and soup mix in small bowl, gradually add 2 cups (500 ml) water and stir until they mix well. Pour over roast.

Cover and cook on LOW for 7 to 8 hours or until roast is tender. Serves 6 to 8.

TIP: This is a great gravy to serve over mashed potatoes. Use instant mashed potatoes. They will never know the difference and will love the meal!

Removing the lid of a slow cooker will cause heat to escape. It will take approximately 20 minutes for the cooker to bring the heat back to the level it was before the lid was lifted.

Beef in Burgundy Sauce

- 1 (2 - 3 pound) beef chuck roast, cubed   910 g - 1.4 kg
- ½ cup flour   60 g
- 1 tablespoon olive oil   15 ml
- 1 onion, sliced
- 1 (10 ounce) package button mushrooms, sliced   280 g
- 1 cup burgundy wine   250 ml
- 1 (10 ounce) can beef broth   280 g
- ½ cup minced fresh parsley   30 g
- 1 clove garlic, minced
- 2 bay leaves

Season beef with a little salt and pepper. Dredge in flour and brown on all sides in hot oil. Place in slow cooker and add all remaining ingredients.

Cook on LOW for about 6 hours or until roast is tender. Serves 6 to 8.

205

Crocked Beef Roast

- 1 (2 - 3 pound) chuck roast, trimmed — 910 g - 1.4 kg
- 1 cup dry red wine — 250 ml
- ¼ cup ketchup — 70 g
- 2 tablespoons Worcestershire sauce — 30 ml
- 2 tablespoons dijon-style mustard — 30 ml
- 2 cloves garlic, minced
- 4 carrots, sliced
- 2 onions, quartered
- 2 baking potatoes, sliced
- 1 (1 ounce) package brown gravy mix — 30 g

Dredge roast through flour and brown in a little oil in skillet over high heat. Place in sprayed slow cooker. In separate bowl, mix ketchup, Worcestershire, mustard, garlic and ½ cup water and pour over roast.

Mix carrots, onions and potatoes on top of roast and season with a little salt and pepper. Cover and cook on LOW for 6 to 8 hours or until meat is tender.

Remove roast and vegetables and stir in gravy mix. Cook on HIGH for about 15 minutes for gravy to thicken. Serves 6 to 8.

Savory Slow-Cooked Brisket

- 1 (3 - 4 pound) trimmed beef brisket, halved   1.3 - 1.8 kg
- ⅓ cup grape or plum jelly   110 g
- 1 cup ketchup   270 g
- 1 (1 ounce) packet onion soup mix   30 g

Place half of brisket in sprayed slow cooker. Combine jelly, ketchup, onion soup mix and ¾ teaspoon (4 ml) pepper in saucepan and heat just enough to mix well. Spread half over brisket.

Top with remaining brisket and jelly-soup mixture. Cover and cook on LOW for 8 to 9 hours. Slice brisket and serve with cooking juices. Serves 6 to 8.

Smoked Brisket

- 1 (4 - 6 pound) trimmed brisket   1.8 - 2.7 kg
- 1 (4 ounce) bottle liquid smoke   115 g
- Garlic salt
- Celery salt
- Worcestershire sauce
- 1 onion, chopped
- 1 (6 ounce) bottle barbecue sauce   170 g

Place brisket in large shallow dish and pour liquid smoke over top. Sprinkle with garlic salt and celery salt. Cover and refrigerate overnight.

Before cooking, drain liquid smoke and douse brisket with Worcestershire sauce.

Place chopped onion in slow cooker and place brisket on top of onion. Cover and cook on LOW for 7 to 9 hours.

With 1 hour left on cooking time, pour barbecue sauce over brisket and cook for additional 1 hour. Serves 6 to 8.

Seasoned Beef Brisket

- ½ cup packed brown sugar — 110 g
- 1 tablespoon Cajun seasoning — 15 ml
- 2 teaspoons lemon pepper — 10 ml
- 1 tablespoon Worcestershire sauce — 15 ml
- 1 (3 - 4 pound) trimmed beef brisket — 1.3 - 1.8 kg

Combine brown sugar, seasoning, lemon pepper and Worcestershire in small bowl and spread on brisket.

Place brisket in sprayed, oval slow cooker. Cover and cook on LOW for 6 to 8 hours. Serves 6 to 8.

Brisket and Gravy

- 1 (3 - 4 pound) trimmed beef brisket — 1.3 - 1.8 kg
- ¼ cup chili sauce — 70 g
- 1 (1 ounce) packet herb-garlic soup mix — 30 g
- 2 tablespoons Worcestershire sauce — 30 ml
- 3 tablespoons cornstarch — 25 g
- Mashed potatoes

Place beef brisket in sprayed 5 to 6-quart (5 to 6 L) slow cooker. Cut to fit if necessary.

Combine chili sauce, soup mix, Worcestershire and 1½ cups (375 ml) water in bowl and pour over brisket.

Cover and cook on LOW for 9 to 11 hours. Remove brisket and keep warm. Pour juices into 2-cup (500 ml) glass measuring cup and skim fat.

Combine cornstarch and ¼ cup (60 ml) water in saucepan. Add 1½ cups (375 ml) juices and cook, while stirring constantly, until gravy thickens.

Slice beef thinly across grain and serve with mashed potatoes and gravy. Serves 6 to 8.

Shredded Brisket for Sandwiches

- **2 teaspoons onion powder**   **10 ml**
- **1 teaspoon minced garlic**   **5 ml**
- **1 (3 - 4 pound) beef brisket**   **1.3 - 1.8 kg**
- **1 tablespoon liquid smoke**   **15 ml**
- **1 (16 ounce) bottle barbecue sauce**   **455 g**
- **Kaiser rolls or hamburger buns**

Combine onion powder, minced garlic and liquid smoke in bowl and rub over brisket. Place brisket in sprayed, large slow cooker. Add ⅓ cup (75 ml) water to cooker.

Cover and cook on LOW for 6 to 8 hours or until brisket is tender. Remove brisket, cool and reserve ½ cup (125 ml) cooking juices.

Shred brisket with 2 forks and place in large saucepan. Add ½ cup (125 ml) cooking juices and barbecue sauce and heat thoroughly.

Make sandwiches with kaiser rolls or hamburger buns. Serves 6 to 8.

209

The Best Ever Brisket

- **1 (3 - 4) pound fresh, trimmed brisket**   **1.4 - 1.8 kg**
- **3 onions, sliced**
- **1 (8 ounce) package fresh mushrooms, halved**   **225 g**
- **1 teaspoon seasoned salt**   **5 ml**
- **1 (12 ounce) can beer (not light)**   **340 g**
- **1 cup chili sauce**   **270 g**
- **1 (4 ounce) can chopped green chilies**   **115 g**

If necessary, trim brisket to fit into large, sprayed, oval slow cooker. Layer onions and mushrooms in slow cooker and sprinkle with seasoned salt. Top with brisket.

Combine beer, chili sauce and green chilies in medium bowl and mix well. Pour mixture over brisket in slow cooker.

Cover and cook on LOW heat for 10 to 12 hours or on HIGH for 5 to 6 hours. When ready to serve, remove brisket from slow cooker and thinly slice meat across the grain.

Place brisket on serving platter and place onions and mushrooms on top of brisket. Serves 8 to 10.

Orange-Glazed Corned Beef

- **2 onions, sliced**
- **Lemon pepper**
- **1 (3 - 4 pound) seasoned corned beef**   **1.3 - 1.8 kg**

Place sliced onions in sprayed, large slow cooker. Add 1 cup (250 ml) water. Sprinkle lemon pepper liberally over corned beef and place on top on onion.

Cover and cook on LOW for 7 to 9 hours.

Remove corned beef from slow cooker and place in ovenproof pan. Preheat oven to 375° (190° C).

Glaze:

- **¼ cup honey**   **85 g**
- **¼ cup frozen orange juice concentrate, thawed**   **60 ml**
- **1 tablespoon mustard**   **15 ml**

Combining all ingredients in bowl and spoon over corned beef. Bake for 30 minutes and baste occasionally with glaze before serving. Serves 6 to 8.

Beef Short Ribs

- **Flour**
- **3 pounds beef short ribs**   **1.4 kg**
- **3 tablespoons canola oil**   **45 ml**
- **1 onion, thinly sliced**
- **½ cup chili sauce**   **135 g**
- **¼ cup packed brown sugar**   **55 g**
- **3 tablespoons vinegar**   **45 ml**
- **½ teaspoon dry mustard**   **2 ml**
- **1 teaspoon chili powder**   **5 ml**
- **2 tablespoons flour**   **15 g**

Coat ribs with lots of salt and pepper; then dredge in flour, coating well. Brown short ribs in canola oil in large skillet over medium-high heat until they are light brown.

Place onion, chili sauce, brown sugar, vinegar, mustard and chili powder in sprayed slow cooker; mix thoroughly.

Place brown ribs in sprayed slow cooker. Cover and cook on LOW for 6 to 8 hours.

Remove ribs to serving platter and turn slow cooker to HIGH heat. Combine remaining flour with ¾ cup (175 ml) water in bowl and stir into sauce in slow cooker.

Cook for 10 minutes or until mixture thickens. When serving, spoon sauce over ribs. Serves 6.

Beer-Braised Beef Short Ribs

- **2½ - 3 pounds beef short ribs**   **1.1 - 1.4 kg**
- **½ cup flour, divided**   **60 g**
- **1 teaspoon prepared mustard**   **5 ml**
- **2 tablespoons extra-virgin olive oil**
- **2 onions, sliced**
- **2 cloves garlic, minced**
- **1 (12 ounce) bottle lager**   **2 (355 ml)**
- **2 - 3 tablespoons flour**   **15 - 25 g**

Season short ribs with salt and pepper and spread mustard on outside. Set 2 to 3 tablespoons (30 to 45 ml) flour to one side and use remaining flour for ribs.

Dredge ribs in flour and brown in hot oil. Place in slow cooker and add onions, garlic and beer. Cook on LOW for about 8 hours or until ribs are tender.

Remove ribs and onions to oven-proof dish and keep warm in oven. Sprinkle 2 to 3 tablespoons (30 to 45 ml) flour into slow cooker and cook on HIGH for about 10 minutes.

Stir until juices thicken into gravy. Serve with ribs. Serves about 4.

Tender Beef Ribs

- **4 pounds beef short ribs**   **1.8 kg**
- **1 onion, sliced**
- **1 (12 ounce) jar beef gravy**   **340 g**
- **1 (1 ounce) packet beef gravy mix**   **30 g**
- **Mashed potatoes**

Place beef ribs in sprayed 6-quart (6 L) slow cooker. Cover with onion and sprinkle with 1 teaspoon (5 ml) pepper.

Combine beef gravy and dry gravy mix in small bowl and pour over ribs and onion.

Cover and cook on LOW for 9 to 11 hours. (The ribs must cook this long on LOW to tenderize.) Serves 4 to 6.

TIP: Serve with hot mashed potatoes and gravy.

Beef and Noodles al Grande

- 1½ pounds lean ground beef   **680 g**
- 1 (16 ounce) package frozen onions and bell peppers, thawed   **455 g**
- 1 (16 ounce) box Velveeta® cheese, cubed   **455 g**
- 2 (15 ounce) cans Mexican stewed tomatoes with liquid   **425 g**
- 2 (15 ounce) cans whole kernel corn, drained   **2 (425 g)**
- 1 (8 ounce) package medium egg noodles   **225 g**
- 1 cup shredded cheddar cheese   **115 g**
- Fresh parsley or green onions

Brown ground beef in skillet and drain fat.

Place beef in sprayed 5 to 6-quart (5 to 6 L) slow cooker, add onions and peppers, cheese, tomatoes, corn and about 1 teaspoon (5 ml) salt and mix well.

Cover and cook on LOW for 4 to 5 hours.

Cook noodles according to package direction, drain and fold into beef-tomato mixture. Cook for additional 30 minutes to heat thoroughly.

When ready to serve, top with cheddar cheese, several sprinkles of chopped fresh parsley or chopped fresh green onions. Serves 4 to 6.

214

Stuffed Cabbage

- **10 - 12 large cabbage leaves**
- **1½ pounds lean ground beef**   **680 g**
- **½ cup brown rice**   **95 g**
- **1 egg, beaten**
- **¼ teaspoon ground cinnamon**   **1 ml**
- **1 (15 ounce) can tomato sauce**   **425 g**

Wash cabbage leaves, place in saucepan of boiling water and turn off heat. Soak for about 5 minutes.

Remove leaves, drain and cool. Combine beef, rice, egg, 1 teaspoon (5 ml) salt, ½ teaspoon (2 ml) pepper and cinnamon in bowl and mix well.

Place 2 tablespoons (30 ml) beef mixture on each cabbage leaf and roll tightly. (If you can't get 10 to 12 large leaves, put 2 together to make 1 large leaf.)

Stack rolls in sprayed, oval slow cooker and pour tomato sauce over rolls.

Cover and cook on HIGH for 1 hour, lower heat to LOW and cook for additional 6 to 7 hours. Serves 4 to 6.

Southwest Spaghetti

- **1½ pounds lean ground beef**   **680 g**
- **2½ teaspoons chili powder**   **12 ml**
- **1 (15 ounce) can tomato sauce**   **425 g**
- **1 (7 ounce) package spaghetti**   **200 g**
- **1 heaping tablespoon beef seasoning**   **15 ml**
- **Shredded cheddar-Jack cheese**

Brown ground beef in skillet until no longer pink. Place in sprayed 4 to 5-quart (4 to 5 L) slow cooker.

Add chili powder, tomato sauce, spaghetti, 2⅓ cups (575 ml) water and beef seasoning and mix well.

Cover and cook on LOW for 6 to 7 hours. When ready to serve, cover with lots of shredded cheddar-Jack cheese. Serves 4 to 6.

Beef and Gravy

- **2 pounds sirloin steak or thick round steak**   **910 g**
- **Canola oil**
- **1 (1 ounce) packet onion soup mix**   **30 g**
- **1 (10 ounce) can golden mushroom soup**   **280 g**
- **1 (4 ounce) can sliced mushrooms, drained**   **115 g**
- **Noodles, cooked**

Cut steak in ½-inch (1.2 cm) pieces. Brown beef in skillet in a little oil and place in sprayed 5 to 6-quart (5 to 6 L) slow cooker.

Combine onion soup mix, mushroom soup, mushrooms and ½ cup (125 ml) water in bowl and mix well. Spoon over top of beef.

Cover and cook on LOW for 7 to 8 hours. Serve over noodles. Serves 4 to 6.

Sauce for Fancy Meatballs

- **1 (16 ounce) can whole-berry cranberry sauce**   **455 g**
- **1 cup ketchup**   **270 g**
- **⅔ cup packed brown sugar**   **150 g**
- **½ cup beef broth**   **125 ml**
- **1 (18 ounce) package frozen meatballs, thawed**   **510 g**

Combine cranberry sauce, ketchup, brown sugar and broth in sprayed, large slow cooker.

Turn heat to HIGH and let mixture come to a boil for 30 minutes to 1 hour. Place package of thawed meatballs in sauce.

Cover and cook on LOW for 2 hours. Remove meatballs to serving dish with slotted spoon. Insert toothpicks for easy pick up.

Serve as an appetizer, for supper or buffet pick-up food. Serves 4 to 6.

Recipes in this cookbook may be cooked in 3 to 6-quart slow cookers. You may need to adjust the quantity of ingredients for a smaller cooker.

Make-Believe Lasagna

- 1 pound lean ground beef   455 g
- 1 onion, chopped
- ½ teaspoon garlic powder   2 ml
- 1 (18 ounce) can spaghetti sauce   510 g
- ½ teaspoon ground oregano   2 ml
- 6 - 8 lasagna noodles, divided
- 1 (12 ounce) carton cottage cheese, divided   340 g
- ½ cup grated parmesan cheese, divided   50 g
- 1 (12 ounce) package shredded mozzarella cheese, divided   340 g

Brown ground beef and onion in large skillet. Add garlic powder, spaghetti sauce and oregano. Cook just until thoroughly warm.

Spoon layer of meat sauce in sprayed, oval slow cooker. Add layer lasagna noodles (break to fit slow cooker).

Top with layer of half remaining meat sauce, half cottage cheese, half parmesan cheese and half mozzarella cheese. Repeat layers and start with more lasagna noodles.

Cover and cook on LOW for 6 to 8 hours. Serves 4 to 6.

Mac Cheese Supper

- 1½ pounds lean ground beef   680 g
- 2 (7 ounce) packages macaroni and cheese dinners   2 (200 g)
- 1 (15 ounce) can whole kernel corn, drained   425 g
- 1½ cups shredded Monterey Jack cheese   170 g

Sprinkle ground beef with 1 teaspoon (5 ml) salt, brown in skillet until no longer pink and drain.

Prepare macaroni and cheese according to package directions. Spoon in beef, macaroni and corn in sprayed 5-quart (5 L) slow cooker and mix well.

Cover and cook on LOW for 4 to 5 hours.

When ready to serve, sprinkle Jack cheese over top and leave in cooker until cheese melts. Serves 4 to 6.

Hearty Meatloaf Meal

- 1½ - 2 pounds lean ground beef   680 - 910 g
- 1 (1 ounce) packet beefy onion soup mix   30 g
- ⅔ cup quick-cooking oats   55 g
- 2 eggs
- 1 (12 ounce) bottle chili sauce, divided   340 g

Make foil handles for slow cooker (see page 186).

Combine beef, onion soup mix, oats, eggs, ¾ cup (204 g) chili sauce and 1 teaspoon (5 ml) pepper in bowl and mix well.

Shape meat mixture into round ball, place in sprayed slow cooker and pat down into loaf shape.

Cover and cook on LOW for 3 to 4 hours. Before last half hour of cooking time, spread remaining chili sauce over top of loaf and continue cooking.

Use foil handles to lift meatloaf out of slow cooker. Serves 4 to 6.

Cheese-Toppped Meatloaf

- **2 pounds lean ground beef**   **910 g**
- **2 eggs**
- **1 onion, chopped**
- **½ cup chili sauce**   **135 g**
- **1¼ cups seasoned breadcrumbs**   **150 g**
- **1 (8 ounce) package shredded Monterey Jack cheese, divided**   **225 g**

Make foil handles for slow cooker (see page 186). Combine beef, eggs, onion, chili sauce and breadcrumbs in bowl and mix well.

Shape half beef mixture into flat loaf and place in sprayed slow cooker. Sprinkle half cheese over meatloaf and press into meat.

Form remaining meat mixture in same shape as first layer, place over cheese and seal seams. Cover and cook on LOW for 6 to 7 hours.

When ready to serve, sprinkle remaining cheese over loaf and leave in cooker until cheese melts.

Carefully remove loaf with foil handles and place on serving plate. Serves 4 to 6.

Hash Brown Dinner

• 1½ pounds lean ground chuck, browned	680 g
• 1 (1 ounce) packet brown gravy mix	30 g
• 1 (15 ounce) can cream-style corn	425 g
• 1 (15 ounce) can whole kernel corn	425 g
• 1 (8 ounce) package shredded cheddar cheese, divided	225 g
• 1 (18 ounce) package frozen hash browns, partially thawed	510 g
• 1 (10 ounce) can golden mushroom soup	280 g
• 1 (5 ounce) can evaporated milk	150 ml

Place browned beef in sprayed slow cooker and toss with dry brown gravy.

Add cream-style corn and whole kernel corn and cover with half cheddar cheese.

Top with hash browns and remaining cheese. Combine mushroom soup and evaporated milk in bowl. Mix well and pour over hash browns and cheese.

Cover and cook on LOW for 6 to 8 hours. Serves 4 to 6.

Fiesta Beef and Rice

• 1½ pounds lean ground beef	680 g
• 1 (15 ounce) can Mexican stewed tomatoes	425 g
• 1 (7 ounce) box beef-flavored rice mix	200 g
• 1 (11 ounce) can Mexicorn®, drained	310 g
• Salsa	

Sprinkle salt and pepper over ground beef and shape into small patties.

Place in sprayed 5-quart (5 L) oval slow cooker.

Combine stewed tomatoes, rice, corn and 2 cups (500 ml) water in bowl and mix well. Spoon over beef patties.

Cover and cook on LOW for 4 to 5 hours. When ready to serve, place large spoonful of salsa on each serving. Serves 4 to 6.

Beef, Beans and Potatoes

• 1½ pounds lean ground beef	680 g
• 2 onions, coarsely chopped	
• 5 medium potatoes, peeled, sliced	
• 1 (15 ounce) can kidney beans, rinsed, drained	425 g
• 1 (15 ounce) can pinto beans, drained	425 g
• 1 (15 ounce) can Mexican stewed tomatoes	425 g
• 1 (10 ounce) can tomato soup	280 g
• ½ teaspoon basil	2 ml
• ½ teaspoon oregano	2 ml
• 2 teaspoons minced garlic	10 ml

Sprinkle beef with some salt and pepper, brown in skillet and drain. Place onions in sprayed slow cooker and spoon beef over onions.

On top of beef, layer potatoes, kidney and pinto beans. Pour stewed tomatoes and tomato soup over beans and potatoes and sprinkle with basil, oregano and garlic.

Cover and cook on LOW for 7 to 8 hours. Serves 4 to 6.

Meat and Potatoes

• 4 medium potatoes, peeled, sliced	
• 1¼ pounds lean ground beef, browned	570 g
• 1 onion, sliced	
• 1 (10 ounce) can cream of mushroom soup	280 g
• 1 (10 ounce) can vegetable beef soup	280 g

Layer all ingredients with a little salt and pepper in sprayed, large slow cooker. Cover and cook on LOW for 5 to 6 hours. Serves 4 to 6.

Fish is seldom recommended for a slow cooker because it cooks rapidly. Vegetables and sauce for a fish recipe can be prepared in the slow cooker and the fish added in the last 20 to 30 minutes of cooking.

Cheeseburger Supper

- 1 (5 ounce) box bacon and cheddar scalloped potatoes ... 145 g
- ⅓ cup milk ... 75 ml
- ¼ cup (½ stick) butter, melted ... 60 g
- 1½ pounds lean ground beef ... 680 g
- 1 onion, coarsely chopped
- Canola oil
- 1 (15 ounce) can whole kernel corn with liquid ... 425 g
- 1 (8 ounce) package shredded cheddar cheese ... 225 g

Place scalloped potatoes in sprayed slow cooker. Pour 2¼ cups (560 ml) boiling water, milk and butter over potatoes.

Brown ground beef and onion in little oil in skillet, drain and spoon over potatoes. Top with corn.

Cover and cook on LOW for 6 to 7 hours. When ready to serve, sprinkle cheese over corn. Serves 4 to 6.

Beef and Macaroni Supper

- 1 (10 ounce) package macaroni, cooked, drained ... 280 g
- 3 tablespoons canola oil ... 45 ml
- 1½ pounds lean ground beef, browned, drained ... 680 g
- 1 onion, chopped
- 3 ribs celery, chopped
- 2 (10 ounce) cans tomato soup ... 2 (280 g)
- 1 (6 ounce) can tomato paste ... 170 g
- 1 teaspoon beef bouillon granules ... 5 ml
- 1 (8 ounce) package cubed Velveeta® cheese ... 225 g

Toss cooked macaroni with oil to make sure macaroni does not stick together.

Place in sprayed slow cooker. Add beef, onion, celery, tomato soup, tomato paste, beef bouillon and ⅔ cup (150 ml) water and stir to mix well.

Cover and cook on LOW for 4 to 6 hours. Before last hour of cooking time, stir in cubed cheese. Serves 4 to 6.

Beef-Bean Medley

- **1 pound lean ground beef**   455 g
- **1 onion, chopped**
- **6 slices bacon, cooked, crumbled**
- **2 (15 ounce) cans pork and beans**   2 (425 g)
- **1 (15 ounce) can butter beans, rinsed, drained**   425 g
- **1 (15 ounce) can kidney beans, rinsed, drained**   425 g
- **¼ cup ketchup**   70 g
- **¼ cup packed brown sugar**   70 g
- **3 tablespoons vinegar**   45 ml
- **1 (13 ounce) bag original corn chips**   370 g
- **1 (8 ounce) package shredded cheddar cheese**   225 g

Brown ground beef and onion in skillet, drain and transfer to sprayed 4 to 5-quart (4 to 5 L) slow cooker.

Add bacon and all 4 cans of beans. Combine ketchup, brown sugar and vinegar in bowl. Add to cooker and stir.

Cover and cook on LOW for 4 to 6 hours.

When ready to serve, spoon over corn chips and sprinkle cheese over top. Serves 4 to 6.

Beefy Stuffed Shells

- 20 - 22 jumbo past shells
- 1 pound lean ground beef, browned, drained   **455 g**
- ½ cup finely chopped onion   **80 g**
- 1 cup shredded cheddar cheese   **115 g**
- ½ cup seasoned breadcrumbs   **60 g**
- 1 teaspoon minced garlic   **5 ml**
- 1 teaspoon Italian seasoning   **5 ml**
- 2 eggs, beaten
- 2 (26 ounce) jar spaghetti sauce   **2 (740 g)**
- ½ cup shredded mozzarella cheese   **60 g**

Cook pasta shells for 7 minutes in boiling water in saucepan (they need only be partially cooked), drain and place on sheet of wax paper.

Combine beef, onion, cheddar cheese, breadcrumbs, garlic, seasoning and eggs in bowl. Carefully stuff partially cooked pasta shells with spoonful of meat mixture.

Pour 1 jar spaghetti sauce in sprayed slow cooker. Transfer stuffed shells on top of sauce. Pour remaining sauce evenly over pasta. Sprinkle with mozzarella cheese.

Cover and cook on LOW heat for 4 to 5 hours. Do not overcook. Serves 4 to 6.

Italian Tortellini

• ½ pound ground round steak	**225 g**
• 1 (1 pound) package bulk Italian sausage	**455 g**
• 1 (15 ounce) carton refrigerated marinara sauce	**425 g**
• 1 (15 ounce) can Italian stewed tomatoes with liquid	**425 g**
• 1½ cups sliced fresh mushrooms	**110 g**
• 1 (9 ounce) package refrigerated cheese tortellini	**255 g**
• 1½ cups shredded mozzarella cheese	**170 g**

Brown and cook ground beef and sausage in large skillet for about 10 minutes on medium-low heat and drain.

Combine meat mixture, marinara sauce, tomatoes and mushrooms in sprayed 4 to 5-quart (4 to 5 L) slow cooker.

Cover and cook on LOW 6 to 8 hours. Stir in tortellini and sprinkle with mozzarella cheese.

Turn cooker to HIGH and continue cooking for additional 10 to 15 minutes or until tortellini is tender. Serves 4 to 6.

Cooking time on HIGH equals about half the cooking time on LOW.

Tomato Penne

- **2 pounds lean ground beef**   910 g
- **1 large onion, chopped**
- **1 green bell pepper, seeded chopped**
- **1 teaspoon mince garlic**   5 ml
- **1 (15 ounce) can tomato sauce**   425 g
- **1 (15 ounce) can Italian stewed tomatoes**   425 g
- **2 teaspoons Italian seasoning**   10 ml
- **1 (16 ounce) package penne pasta**   455 g
- **1 (10 ounce) package frozen chopped spinach, thawed***   280 g
- **1 (12 ounce) package shredded mozzarella cheese**   340 g

Brown and cook ground beef, onion, bell pepper and garlic in large skillet for about 15 minutes. Drain and place mixture in sprayed slow cooker.

Stir in tomato sauce, stewed tomatoes, Italian seasoning and a little salt and pepper. Cover and cook on LOW for 7 to 8 hours or on HIGH for 3 hours 30 minutes.

Cook pasta according to package directions and drain. Last 30 minutes of cooking time, turn heat to HIGH (if cooking on LOW) stir in pasta, spinach and cheese and continue cooking. Serves 6 to 8.

TIP: Squeeze spinach between paper towels to complete remove excess moisture.

Sloppy Joes

• 3 pounds ground beef	**1.3 kg**
• 1 tablespoon minced garlic	**15 ml**
• 1 large onion, finely chopped	
• 2 ribs celery, chopped	
• ¼ cup packed brown sugar	**55 g**
• 3½ tablespoons mustard	**55 g**
• 1 tablespoon chili powder	**15 ml**
• 1½ cups ketchup	**410 g**
• 3 tablespoons Worcestershire sauce	**45 ml**

Brown beef, garlic and onion in very large skillet and drain. Combine celery, brown sugar, mustard, chili powder, ketchup and Worcestershire in sprayed 5-quart (5 L) slow cooker.

Stir in meat mixture. Cover and cook on LOW heat for 6 to 7 hours. Serves 6 to 8.

TIP: This will make enough to fill 16 to 18 hamburger buns.

Special Hot Dog Supper

- 1 pound beef wieners   455 g
- 2 (15 ounce) cans chili without beans   2 (425 g)
- 1 onion, finely chopped
- 1 (10 ounce) can cheddar cheese soup   280 g
- 1 (10 ounce) can fiesta nacho cheese soup   280 g
- 1 (7 ounce) can chopped green chilies, drained   200 g
- Corn chips or tortilla chips

Cut wieners in ½-inch (1.2 cm) pieces and place in sprayed slow cooker.

Combine chili, onion, cheese soup, nacho cheese soup and green chilies in saucepan. (Omit green chilies if serving to kids.)

Heat just enough to mix ingredients well. Spoon over wieners. Cover and cook on LOW for 1 hour 30 minutes to 2 hours.

Serve over bowl of small corn chips or crisp tortilla chips slightly crushed. Serves 4 to 6.

Pork Main Dishes

Pork Chops with Mushroom Gravy

- **1 (10 ounce) can cream of mushroom soup**   **280 g**
- **1 (4 ounce) can sliced mushrooms**   **115 g**
- **5 - 6 boneless pork chops**
- **Lemon pepper**
- **2 (15 ounce) cans whole new potatoes, drained**   **2 (425 g)**
- **1 (10 ounce) can frozen green peas, thawed**   **280 g**

Spoon soup and mushrooms in sprayed slow cooker and stir in ¼ cup (60 ml) water to thin soup slightly.

Season each pork chop with lemon pepper and place in slow cooker. Cover and cook on LOW for 6 to 8 hours.

Remove lid and place potatoes and peas around pork chops; turn heat to HIGH and cook for additional 1 hour 30 minutes. Serves 5.

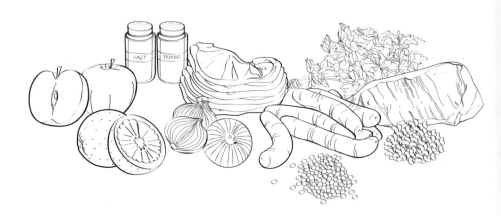

Stuffed Pork Chops

- **6 (1 inch) thick boneless pork chops**   **6 (2.5 cm)**
- **1 teaspoon seasoned salt**   **5 ml**
- **1 (11 ounce) can Mexicorn®, drained**   **310 g**
- **1 (10 ounce) package frozen chopped onions and bell peppers, thawed**   **280 g**
- **1 (4 ounce) can sliced mushrooms, drained, chopped**   **115 g**
- **1¼ cups seasoned breadcrumbs**   **150 g**
- **1 (8 ounce) can tomato sauce**   **225 g**
- **1 (4 ounce) can chopped green chilies**   **115 g**

Cut pocket in each pork chop, cutting from side almost to edge. Season pockets with seasoned salt.

Combine corn, onions and bell peppers, mushrooms and breadcrumbs in bowl. Pack vegetable mixture into pockets and secure along open side with toothpicks.

Spread any remaining vegetable mixture in sprayed slow cooker. Combine tomato sauce and green chilies in bowl and mix well.

Moisten top surface of each stuffed chop with tomato mixture and place in slow cooker. Pour remaining tomato mixture on top of pork chops.

Cover and cook on LOW for 8 to 9 hours or on HIGH for 4 to 5 hours. When ready to serve, remove pork chops to serving platter and mound vegetable mixture in center. Serves 6.

Onion Ring-Topped Pork Chops

- **6 (¾ inch) thick bone-in pork chops**   6 (1.8 cm)
- **8 - 10 medium red (new) potatoes with peels**
- **2 onions, sliced**
- **1 (10 ounce) can cream of chicken soup**   280 g
- **1 (10 ounce) can chicken broth**   280 g
- **¼ cup dijon-style mustard**   60 g
- **1 teaspoon dried basil leaves**   5 ml
- **1 (3 ounce) can fried onion rings**

Brown pork chops sprinkled with a little salt and pepper in non-stick skillet. Place potatoes and onions in sprayed slow cooker and add browned pork chops.

Combine soup, mustard and basil leaves in saucepan. Heat just enough to mix well and pour over pork chops.

Cover and cook on LOW for 7 to 9 hours. Top with onion rings before serving. Serves 4 to 6.

Savory Pork Chops

- **6 (¾ inch) thick pork chops**   6 (1.8 cm)
- **1 cup pineapple juice**   250 ml
- **⅓ cup packed brown sugar**   75 g
- **3 tablespoons cider vinegar**   45 ml
- **Noodles, cooked**

Brown pork chops in skillet on both sides and place in sprayed 5-quart (5 L) slow cooker.

Combine pineapple juice, brown sugar and vinegar in bowl and mix well.

Pour brown sugar-vinegar mixture over pork chops. Cover and cook on LOW for 4 to 5 hours. Serve over noodles. Serves 4 to 6.

Ranch Pork Chops

- **6 (¾ inch) thick bone-in pork chops**   **6 (1.8 cm)**
- **1 (.04 ounce) packet ranch dressing mix**   **10 g**
- **2 (15 ounce) cans new potatoes, drained, quartered**   **2 (425 g)**
- **1 (10 ounce) can French onion soup**   **280 g**

Place pork chops in sprayed 6-quart (6 L) oval slow cooker. Sprinkle pork chops with ranch dressing mix and ½ teaspoon (2 ml) pepper.

Place potatoes around pork chops and pour French onion soup around potatoes and chops. Cover and cook on LOW for 4 to 5 hours. Serves 4 to 6.

Pork Chops with Orange Sauce

- **2 medium sliced yellow squash**
- **2 onions, sliced**
- **6 - 8 bone-in pork chops**
- **½ cup chicken broth**   **125 ml**
- **½ cup orange marmalade**   **160 g**
- **1 tablespoon honey-mustard**   **15 ml**
- **2 tablespoons cornstarch**   **15 g**

Place squash and onions in sprayed 5 to 6-quart (5 to 6 L) slow cooker. Sprinkle a little salt and pepper on top of pork chops and place over vegetables.

Combine broth, marmalade and mustard in bowl and spoon over pork chops. Cover and cook on LOW for 4 to 6 hours.

Transfer pork chops and vegetables to serving plate and cover to keep warm.

For sauce, pour liquid from slow cooker into medium saucepan. Combine 2 tablespoons (30 ml) water with cornstarch and add to saucepan.

Heat mixture, stir constantly until thick and serve over pork chops and vegetables. Serves 6 to 8.

Western Pork Supper

- **6 (¾ inch) pork loin chops** — 6 (1.8 cm)
- **1 (15 ounce) can chili beans** — 425 g
- **1½ cups salsa** — 395 g
- **1 (16 ounce) package frozen seasoned corn with black beans, tomatoes, bell peppers, onions, thawed** — 455 g
- **1 (4 ounce) can sliced ripe olives** — 115 g
- **1½ - 2 cups instant brown rice** — 145 - 190 g
- **2 tablespoons butter, melted** — 30 g

Arrange pork chops in sprayed, oval slow cooker and cover with chili beans and salsa. Cover and cook on LOW for 5 hours or on HIGH for 2 hours 30 minutes.

Increase heat to HIGH (if cooking on LOW) and stir in seasoned corn. Cover and cook for additional 30 minutes.

Cook brown rice according to package directions and stir in melted butter. Place on serving platter. Spoon pork chops and vegetables over rice.

Barbecue-Style Pork Chops

- **6 (¾ inch) thick pork loin chops** — 6 (1.8 cm)
- **1 onion, halved, sliced**
- **1 (8 ounce) can tomato sauce** — 225 g
- **¼ cup packed brown sugar** — 55 g
- **1 tablespoon Worcestershire sauce** — 15 ml
- **1 teaspoon seasoned salt** — 5 ml

Brown pork chops in skillet on both sides and place in sprayed 4 to 5-quart (4 to 5 L) slow cooker. Place onions over pork chops.

Combine tomato sauce, brown sugar, Worcestershire sauce, seasoned salt and ¼ cup (60 ml) water in bowl and spoon over onions and pork chops.

Cover and cook on LOW for 4 to 5 hours. Serves 4 to 6.

Pork Chops and Gravy

- **6 (½ inch) thick pork chops** — **6 (1.2 cm)**
- **8 - 10 new (red) potatoes with peels, quartered**
- **1 (16 ounce) package baby carrots** — **455 g**
- **2 (10 ounce) cans cream of mushroom soup with roasted garlic** — **2 (280 g)**

Sprinkle a little salt and pepper on pork chops. Brown pork chops in skillet and place in sprayed 5 to 6-quart (5 to 6 L) slow cooker. Place potatoes and carrots around pork chops.

Heat mushroom soup with ½ cup (125 ml) water in saucepan and pour over chops and vegetables.

Cover and cook on LOW for 6 to 7 hours. Serves 4 to 6.

Pizza Pork Chops

- **6 (1 inch) thick boneless pork chops** — **6 (2.5 cm)**
- **1 onion, finely chopped**
- **1 green bell pepper, seeded, finely chopped**
- **1 (8 ounce) jar pizza sauce** — **225 g**
- **1 (10 ounce) box plain couscous** — **280 g**
- **2 tablespoons butter** — **30 g**
- **1 cup shredded mozzarella cheese** — **115 g**

Trim fat from pork chops and sprinkle with a little salt and pepper. Brown and cook pork chops in skillet on both sides for 5 minutes.

Transfer chops to sprayed, oval slow cooker. Spoon onion and bell pepper over chops and pour pizza sauce over top. Cover and cook on LOW for 4 to 6 hours.

Cook couscous according to package directions except add 2 tablespoons (28 g) butter instead of 1 tablespoon (15 ml) and place on serving platter.

Spoon chops and sauce over couscous and sprinkle cheese over chops. Serves 4 to 6.

Creamy Pork Chops with Penne

- **6 boneless pork chops**
- **1 (4 ounce) can sliced mushrooms**   115 g
- **1 (7 ounce) can tomatoes and green chilies**   200 g
- **1 (10 ounce) can cream of mushroom soup**   280 g
- **1 (8 ounce) carton sour cream**   225 g
- **1 (8 ounce) package penne pasta**   225 g

Place pork chops in sprayed 5-quart (5 L) slow cooker and layer mushrooms, tomatoes and green chilies over top. Spread mushroom soup with large spoon over top.

Cover and cook on LOW for 6 to 8 hours. Transfer pork chops to container that can be kept warm in oven.

Stir sour cream into sauce in slow cooker and cook on HIGH for about 10 minutes.

Cook pasta according to package directions. Stir pasta into sauce and place pork chops on top.

If you prefer, place pasta-sauce on serving platter and top with warm pork chops. Serves 6.

Pineapple-Pork Chops

- 6 - 8 (½ inch) thick boneless pork chops   6 - 8 (1.2 cm)
- Canola oil
- 1 (6 ounce) can frozen pineapple juice concentrate, thawed   170 g
- ¼ cup packed brown sugar   55 g
- ⅓ cup wine or tarragon vinegar   75 ml
- ⅓ cup honey   115 g
- 1 (6 ounce) package parmesan-butter rice, cooked   170 g

Brown pork chops in a little oil in skillet and transfer to sprayed slow cooker.

Combine pineapple juice concentrate, brown sugar, vinegar and honey in bowl. Pour over pork chops.

Cover and cook on LOW for 5 to 6 hours. Serve over rice. Serves 6 to 8.

5-Minute Pork Chops

- 1¾ cups flour   210 g
- Scant 2 tablespoons dry mustard   30 ml
- 8 boneless, thick pork chops
- Canola oil
- 1 (10 ounce) can chicken and rice soup   280 g

Place flour and mustard in shallow bowl. Dredge pork chops in flour-mustard mixture.

Brown pork chops in a little oil in skillet. Place all chops in sprayed 6-quart (6 L) oval slow cooker.

Pour soup over pork and add about ¼ cup (60 ml) water. Cover and cook on LOW for 6 to 8 hours. Serves 6 to 8.

Peachy Pork Chops

- **6 - 8 (¾ inch) thick bone-in pork chops** 1.8 cm
- **½ cup packed brown sugar** 110 g
- **¼ teaspoon ground cinnamon** 1 ml
- **¼ teaspoon ground cloves** 1 ml
- **1 (8 ounce) can tomato sauce** 225 g
- **1 (28 ounce) can peach halves with juice** 795 g
- **¼ cup white vinegar** 60 ml

Brown pork chops in skillet on both sides and place in sprayed, oval slow cooker.

Combine brown sugar, cinnamon, cloves, tomato sauce, ¼ cup (60 ml) juice from peaches and vinegar in bowl.

Pour sugar-tomato sauce mixture over pork chops and place peach halves over top. Cover and cook on LOW for 4 to 5 hours. Serves 6 to 8.

Italian Pork Chops

- **6 - 8 (1 inch) thick boneless pork chops** 6 - 8 (2.5 cm)
- **½ pound fresh mushrooms, sliced** 225 g
- **1 (10 ounce) package frozen onion-bell pepper blend, thawed** 280 g
- **1 teaspoon Italian seasoning** 5 ml
- **1 (15 ounce) can Italian stewed tomatoes** 425 g

Brown pork chops in skillet and sprinkle with salt and pepper on both sides.

Combine mushrooms, onion-bell pepper blend and Italian seasoning in sprayed 6-quart (6 L) slow cooker and set aside.

Place pork chops over vegetables and pour stewed tomatoes over pork chops. Cover and cook on LOW for 7 to 8 hours.

To serve, spoon mushroom-seasoning blend over pork chops. Serves 6 to 8.

Honey-Mustard Pork Chops

Try this sauce over hot, cooked rice. It is wonderful!

• 1 (10 ounce) can golden mushroom soup	280 g
• ⅓ cup white wine	75 ml
• ¼ cup honey-mustard	60 g
• 1 teaspoon minced garlic	5 ml
• 4 - 5 (¾ inch) thick pork chops	1.8 cm

Combine soup, wine, honey-mustard, minced garlic and 1 teaspoon (5 ml) salt in large bowl and mix well.

Place pork chops, sprinkled with a little black pepper in sprayed 5-quart (5 L) slow cooker and spoon soup-honey-mustard mixture over chops.

Cover and cook on LOW for 5 to 6 hours.

When ready to serve, lift pork chops out of sauce and onto serving plate. Stir sauce to mix well and serve with chops. Serves 4 to 5.

TIP: For a "meat and potato meal", just slice 3 potatoes and place in slow cooker before adding pork chops.

"Baked" Pork Chops

• 6 - 8 (½ inch) thick pork chops	1.2 cm
• Canola oil	
• 1 (10 ounce) can cream of chicken soup	280 g
• 3 tablespoons ketchup	50 g
• 1 tablespoon Worcestershire sauce	15 ml
• 1 onion, chopped	

Brown pork chops in a little oil in skillet and season with a little salt and pepper.

Place pork chops in sprayed slow cooker. Combine chicken soup, ketchup, Worcestershire and onion in bowl and pour over pork chops.

Cover and cook on LOW for 5 to 6 hours. Serves 6 to 8.

Country Pork Chops

- 7 - 8 new (red) potatoes with peels, sliced
- 2 onions, sliced
- 1 (10 ounce) can cream of celery soup   280 g
- ⅓ cup chicken broth   75 ml
- 3 tablespoons dijon-style mustard   45 ml
- 1 (4 ounce) can sliced mushrooms, drained   115 g
- 1 teaspoon minced garlic   5 ml
- ¾ teaspoon dried basil   4 ml
- 8 boneless pork chops
- Canola oil

Place potatoes and onions in sprayed, large slow cooker. Combine soup, broth, mustard, mushrooms, garlic and basil in bowl, mix well and pour over potatoes and onions. Stir to coat vegetables.

Sprinkle pork chops with a little salt and pepper. Brown pork chops in a little oil in skillet on both sides.

Place chops over vegetables. Cover and cook on LOW for 6 to 7 hours. Serves 6 to 8.

Pork Chops Dijon

- ¼ cup dijon-style mustard   60 g
- 4 - 6 (1 inch) pork chops   4 -6 (2.5 cm)
- Flour
- 2 cloves garlic, minced
- 8 small red potatoes, quartered
- 1 onion, chopped

Spread mustard over pork chops and dredge each through flour. Brown chops in skillet with hot oil over high heat on both sides.

Place in slow cooker and sprinkle garlic, potatoes and onions on top. Cover and cook on LOW for 6 to 8 hours or until pork chops are no longer pink on the inside. Serves 4.

Pork Roast with Apricot Glaze

- 1 (3 pound) boneless pork roast   **1.3 kg**
- ⅓ cup chicken broth   **75 ml**
- 1 (18 ounce) jar apricot preserves   **510 g**
- 2 tablespoons dijon-style mustard   **30 g**
- 1 onion, finely chopped
- 1 green bell pepper, seeded, finely chopped
- Rice, cooked

Trim fat from roast and, if necessary, cut roast to fit into sprayed 4 to 5-quart (4 to 5 L) slow cooker. Place in roast in cooker.

Combine broth, preserves, mustard, onion and bell pepper in saucepan and heat just enough to mix ingredients well and pour over roast.

Cover and cook on LOW for 9 to 10 hours or on HIGH for 5 to 6 hours.

Transfer meat to serving plate. Sauce left in cooker is delicious as is or thicker.

To thicken sauce, mix 1 tablespoon (15 ml) cornstarch and 2 tablespoons (30 ml) water. Place in saucepan and add sauce from cooker.

Heat sauce and stir constantly until sauce thickens slightly. Sauce may be served with rice or just spoon over roast. Serves 6 to 8.

Cinnamon-Sugared Pork Roast

- **1 (2½ - 3 pound) pork roast**   **1.1 - 1.4 kg**
- **Flour**
- **¼ cup packed brown sugar**   **55 g**
- **¼ cup soy sauce**   **60 ml**
- **2 gala apples**
- **¼ cup sugar**   **50 g**
- **2 tablespoons cinnamon**   **30 ml**

Dredge pork roast in flour and brown on all sides in hot oil in skillet over high heat. Place in slow cooker.

Mix brown sugar, soy sauce and ½ cup (125 ml) water in saucepan and cook over low heat until sugar dissolves; stir frequently. Pour over roast, cover and cook on LOW for 8 hours.

Peel, core and slice apples and place in large bowl. Pour sugar and cinnamon on top and make sure sugar and cinnamon stick to apple slices. Add to roast and cook 1 hour. Serves 6 to 8.

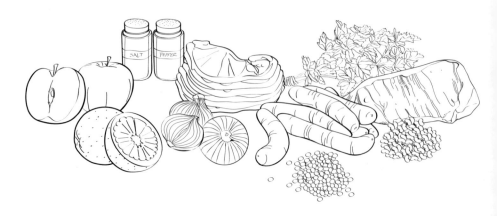

Showtime Pork Roast

- **2 onions, sliced**
- **1 green bell pepper, seeded, sliced**
- **3 pound boneless pork roast**   **1.3 kg**
- **2 tablespoons soy sauce**   **30 ml**
- **1 tablespoon ketchup**   **15 ml**
- **¼ cup sugar**   **50 g**
- **3 tablespoons red wine vinegar**   **45 ml**
- **1 teaspoon minced garlic**   **5 ml**
- **1 (12 ounce) package egg noodles, cooked, buttered**   **340 g**

Arrange onion and bell pepper in sprayed slow cooker; then place roast on top.

Combine soy sauce, ketchup, sugar, vinegar, garlic and a little salt in bowl; mix well and pour over roast.

Cover and cook on LOW heat for 6 to 8 hours or on HIGH for 3 to 4 hours. Serve over noodles. Serves 8.

Fruit-Stuffed Pork Roast

• 1 (3 - 3½ pound) boneless pork loin roast	1.3 kg
• 1 cup mixed dried fruits	160 g
• 1 tablespoon dried onion flakes	15 ml
• 1 teaspoon thyme leaves	5 ml
• ½ teaspoon ground cinnamon	2 ml
• 2 tablespoons canola oil	30 ml
• ½ cup apple cider	125 ml

Place pork on cutting board. Cut horizontally through center of pork almost to opposite side. Open pork like a book.

Layer dried fruits and onion flakes in opening. Bring halves of pork together and tie at 1-inch (2.5 cm) intervals with kitchen twine.

Combine ½ teaspoon (2 ml) salt, thyme, cinnamon and ½ teaspoon (2 ml) pepper in small bowl and rub into roast.

Place roast in skillet with oil and brown roast on all sides. Place roast in sprayed slow cooker and pour apple cider in cooker. Cover and cook on LOW for 3 to 4 hours. Partially cool before slicing. Serves 6 to 8.

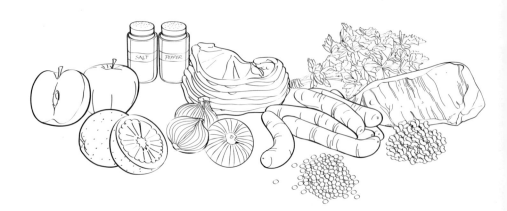

Pork with a Cranberry Glaze

• 1 (3 - 4 pound) pork shoulder roast	1.3 - 1.8 kg
• 1 (16 ounce) package frozen stew vegetables, thawed	455 g
• 1 (16 ounce) can whole cranberry sauce	455 g
• 1 (4 ounce) can chopped green chilies	115 g
• ¾ cup chili sauce	205 g
• 1 teaspoon dijon-style mustard	5 ml
• 2 tablespoons brown sugar	30 g

Brown roast on all sides in sprayed skillet over medium heat. Place roast in sprayed slow cooker and top with stew vegetables.

Combine cranberry sauce, green chilies, chili sauce, mustard and brown sugar in saucepan; heat just enough to blend ingredients. Pour mixture over roast and vegetables.

Cover and cook on LOW heat for 8 to 9 hours or on HIGH for 4 to 4 hours 30 minutes. Transfer roast and vegetables to serving platter and keep warm.

Strain cooking juices and skim off fat. Bring juices to a boil in medium saucepan; reduce heat and simmer for about 25 minutes or until mixture thickens. Serve sauce with sliced pork roast. Serves 6 to 8.

Tender Pork Loin

- 1 (3 - 4 pound) pork loin   1.3 kg
- 2 teaspoons minced garlic   10 ml
- ½ teaspoon rosemary   2 ml
- 1 teaspoon sage   5 ml
- 1½ teaspoons marjoram   7 ml

Place pork loin in sprayed slow cooker, rub with minced garlic and sprinkle with rosemary, sage and marjoram. Add about ¼ cup (60 ml) water to slow cooker.

Cover and cook on LOW heat for 4 to 5 hours. Serves 6 to 8.

TIP: Sometimes it is hard to buy a small (3 to 4 pound/1.3 to 1.8 kg) pork loin, but they are available in (8 to 9 pound/3.6 to 3.8 kg) sizes. Because pork loin is such a good cut of pork (no bones - no fat), you can buy a whole loin, cut it into 2 or 3 pieces and freeze the extra pieces for later use.

Terrific Pork Tenderloin

- 2 - 3 (1 pound) pork tenderloins   2 - 3 (455 g)
- 1 teaspoon seasoned salt   5 ml
- 1 teaspoon garlic powder   5 ml
- 1 (4 ounce) can chopped green chilies   115 g
- 2 (10 ounce) cans cream of celery soup   2 (280 g)
- Rice, cooked

Place tenderloins in sprayed, oval slow cooker. Season with seasoned salt and garlic powder.

Combine green chilies and celery soup in bowl and spoon over tenderloins, covering completely. Cover and cook on LOW for 8 hours. Serve over rice. Serves 2 to 3.

Recipes in this cookbook may be cooked in 3 to 6-quart slow cookers. You may need to adjust the quantity of ingredients for a smaller cooker.

Spinach-Stuffed Pork Roast

- **1 (2 - 2½ pound) pork tenderloin**   **910 g**
- **1 (10 ounce) package frozen chopped spinach, thawed**   **280 g**
- **⅓ cup seasoned breadcrumbs**   **40 g**
- **⅓ cup grated parmesan cheese**   **35 g**
- **2 tablespoons canola oil**   **30 ml**
- **½ teaspoon seasoned salt**   **2 ml**

Cut tenderloin horizontally lengthwise about ½-inch (1.2 cm) from top to within ¾-inch (1.8 cm) of opposite end and open flat.

Turn pork to cut other side, from inside edge to outer edge, and open flat. If one side is thicker than other side, cover with plastic wrap and pound until both sides are ¾-inch (1.8 cm) thick.

Squeeze spinach between paper towels to completely remove excess moisture.

Combine spinach, breadcrumbs and cheese in bowl and mix well. Spread mixture on inside surfaces of pork and press down. Roll pork and tie with kitchen twine.

Heat oil in large skillet over medium-high heat and brown pork on all sides.

Place in sprayed, oval slow cooker and sprinkle with salt. Cover and cook on LOW for 6 to 8 hours. Serves 4 to 6.

Pork and Cabbage Supper

• 1 (16 ounce) package baby carrots	455 g
• 1 cup chicken broth	250 ml
• 1 (1 ounce) packet golden onion soup mix	30 g
• 1 (3 - 4 pound) pork shoulder roast	1.3 - 1.8 kg
• 1 medium head cabbage	

Place carrots in sprayed 5-quart (5 L) slow cooker.

Add chicken broth and 1 cup (250 ml) water. Sprinkle dry soup mix and lots of black pepper over carrots.

Cut roast in half (if needed to fit in cooker) and place over carrot mixture. Cover and cook on LOW for 6 to 7 hours.

Cut cabbage in small-size chunks and place over roast. Cover and cook for additional 1 to 2 hours or until cabbage cooks. Serves 6 to 8.

Home-Style Ribs

• 4 - 6 pounds boneless pork spareribs	1.8 - 2.7 kg
• 1 cup chili sauce	270 g
• 1 cup packed brown sugar	220 g
• 2 tablespoons vinegar	30 ml
• 2 tablespoons Worcestershire sauce	30 ml

Sprinkle ribs liberally with salt and pepper. Place ribs in sprayed slow cooker.

Combine ½ cup (125 ml) water, chili sauce, brown sugar, vinegar and Worcestershire in bowl and spoon over ribs.

Cover and cook on LOW for 5 to 6 hours. Serves 6 to 8.

Do prep work ahead of time and seal chopped veggies, meats, etc., in plastic bags and refrigerate until ready to assemble the food in the slow cooker.

Roasted Red Pepper Tenderloin

- **2 pounds pork tenderloin**   **910 g**
- **1 (.04 ounce) packet ranch dressing mix**   **10 g**
- **1 cup roasted red bell peppers, rinsed, chopped**   **90 g**
- **1 (8 ounce) carton sour cream**   **225 g**

Brown tenderloins in large skillet and place in sprayed 6-quart (6 L) oval slow cooker.

Combine ranch dressing mix, red bell peppers and ½ cup (125 ml) water in bowl and spoon over tenderloins. Cover and cook on LOW for 4 to 5 hours.

When ready to serve, remove tenderloins from slow cooker. Stir sour cream into sauce made. Serve over tenderloin slices. Serves 4 to 6.

Walnut Ham

- **½ pound cooked, ham slices**   **225 g**
- **2 (10 ounce) cans cream of onion soup**   **2 (280 g)**
- **⅓ cup grated parmesan cheese**   **35 g**
- **⅔ cup chopped walnuts**   **90 g**
- **Linguine, cooked**

Cut ham into ½-inch (1.2 cm) strips. Place soups, cheese, walnuts and ham strips in sprayed slow cooker.

Cover and cook on LOW for 1 to 2 hours or until hot and bubbly. Serve over linguine. Serves 4.

Honey-Mustard Pork Roast

- **1 green bell pepper, seeded, chopped**
- **1 red bell pepper, seeded, chopped**
- **2 yellow onions, seeded, chopped**
- **3 tablespoons sweet and tangy honey-mustard** — **45 g**
- **1 (2 - 2 ½ pound) pork loin roast** — **910 g - 1.2 kg**

Combine bell peppers and onions in sprayed 4 to 5-quart (4 to 5 L) slow cooker. Rub honey-mustard liberally over pork loin with most of honey-mustard on top; place in slow cooker.

Cover and cook on LOW for 4 to 6 hours and place in serving platter. Spoon bell peppers, onions and pan juices in small serving bowl and spoon over slices of roast to serve. Serves 4 to 6.

Tender Apricot Ribs

- **4 - 5 pounds baby back pork ribs** — **1.8 - 2.2 kg**
- **1 (16 ounce) jar apricot preserves** — **455 g**
- **⅓ cup soy sauce** — **75 ml**
- **¼ cup packed light brown sugar** — **55 g**
- **2 teaspoons garlic powder** — **10 ml**
- **¼ cup apple cider vinegar** — **60 ml**

Place ribs in sprayed slow cooker. Combine preserves, soy sauce, brown sugar, garlic powder and vinegar in bowl and spoon over ribs.

Cover and cook on LOW for 6 to 7 hours. Serves 8 to 10.

Whenever you buy a roast, ham or large cut of meat, make sure it will fit in the slow cooker. If it is too large, cut it in half to make it fit. The oval shape slow cooker is very versatile and will usually hold the larger cuts.

Ginger Pork

- 1 (2 - 2½ pound) boneless pork roast — 910 g
- 1 cup chicken broth — 250 ml
- 3½ tablespoons quick-cooking tapioca — 50 ml
- 3 tablespoons soy sauce — 45 ml
- 1 teaspoon grated fresh ginger — 5 ml
- 1 (15 ounce) can pineapple chunks with juice — 425 g
- 1 (16 ounce) package baby carrots — 455 g
- 1 (8 ounce) can sliced water chestnuts, drained — 225 g
- Rice, cooked

Trim fat from pork. Cut pork into 1-inch (2.5 cm) pieces, brown in large skillet and drain.

Combine chicken broth, tapioca, soy sauce, ginger, pineapple juice, carrots and water chestnuts in sprayed 4 to 5-quart (4 to 5 L) slow cooker. (Chill pineapple chunks in refrigerator until ready to include in recipe.)

Add browned pork. Cover and cook on LOW for 6 to 8 hours.

Turn heat to HIGH and stir in pineapple chunks. Cover and cook for additional 10 minutes.

Serve over rice. Serves 4 to 6.

251

Barbecue Pork Roast

Use leftovers for great sandwiches.

• 1 onion, thinly sliced	
• 2 tablespoons flour	15 g
• 1 (2 - 3 pound) pork shoulder roast	910 g - 1.3 kg
• 1 (8 ounce) bottle barbecue sauce	225 g
• 1 tablespoon chili powder	15 ml
• 1 teaspoon ground cumin	5 ml

Separate onion slices into rings and place in sprayed 4 to 5-quart (4 to 5 L) slow cooker. Sprinkle flour over onions. If necessary, cut roast to fit cooker and place over onions.

Combine barbecue sauce, chili powder and cumin in bowl and pour over roast.

Cover and cook on LOW for 8 to 10 hours. Remove roast from cooker and slice. Serve sauce over sliced roast. Serves 6 to 8.

TIP: *To make sandwiches, shred roast and return to cooker. Cook for additional 30 minutes to heat thoroughly.*

Finger Lickin' Baby Backs

• 2½ - 3 pounds baby back pork ribs	1.2 - 1.3 kg
• ½ cup chili sauce	135 g
• ⅓ cup apple cider vinegar	75 ml
• ½ cup packed brown sugar	110 g

Cut ribs in serving-size pieces, sprinkle with black pepper and place in sprayed 5 to 6-quart (5 to 6 L) slow cooker.

Combine chili sauce, vinegar, brown sugar and about ¾ cup (175 ml) water in bowl and pour over ribs.

Cover and cook on LOW for about 6 to 7 hours. After about 3 hours, you might move ribs around in slow cooker so sauce is spread over all ribs. Serves 4 to 6.

Zesty Ham Supper

- 1 (28 ounce) package frozen hash-brown potatoes with onions
  and peppers, thawed   795 g
- 3 cups cooked, diced ham   420 g
- 1 (10 ounce) box frozen green peas, thawed   280 g
- 2 (10 ounce) cans fiesta nacho cheese soup   2 (280 g)
- 1 cup milk   250 ml
- 1 bunch fresh green onions, chopped

Place potatoes, ham and peas in sprayed 6-quart (6 L) slow cooker and stir to mix.

Combine soup and milk in bowl and mix well. Pour over potato mixture and mix well. Cover and cook on LOW for 6 to 8 hours.

Sprinkle green onions over top when ready to serve. Serves 6 to 8.

Apricot Ham

- 1 (6 - 8 pound) butt or shank ham   2.7 - 3.6 kg
- Whole cloves
- 2 tablespoons dry mustard   30 g
- 1¼ cups apricot jam   400 g
- 1¼ cups packed light brown sugar   275 g

Place ham, fat-side up in sprayed slow cooker. Stick lots of whole cloves on outside of ham.

Combine mustard, jam and brown sugar in bowl and spread all over ham. Cover and cook on LOW for 5 to 6 hours. Serves 8 to 10.

Tougher or cheaper cuts of meat cook better on LOW in the slow cooker and have a better chance of becoming tender with longer cooking times.

Saucy Ham Loaf

Great with sweet and hot mustard recipe below

- **1 pound ground ham**   **455 g**
- **½ pound ground beef**   **225 g**
- **½ pound ground pork**   **225 g**
- **2 eggs, slightly beaten**
- **1 cup Italian-seasoned breadcrumbs**   **120 g**
- **1 (5 ounce) can evaporated milk**   **150 ml**
- **¼ cup chili sauce**   **70 g**
- **1 teaspoon seasoned salt**   **5 ml**

Combine all ingredients in bowl and form into loaf in sprayed, oval slow cooker. Shape loaf so that neither end touches sides of cooker.

Cover and cook on LOW for 6 to 7 hours. Serve with Sweet-and-Hot Mustard.

Sweet-and-Hot Mustard:

Use on Saucy Ham Loaf or ham sandwiches.

- **4 ounces dry mustard**   **115 g**
- **1 cup vinegar**   **250 ml**
- **3 eggs, beaten**
- **1 cup sugar**   **200 g**

Mix mustard and vinegar in bowl until smooth and let stand overnight.

Add eggs and sugar and cook in double boiler for 8 to 10 minutes or until it coats the spoon. Cool and store in covered jars in refrigerator. Serve with Saucy Ham Loaf. Serves 4 to 6.

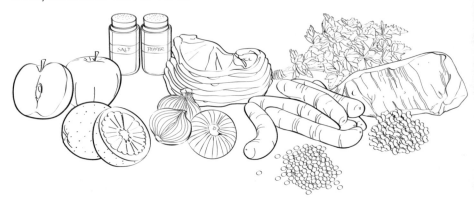

Cherry-Glazed Ham Loaf

Great for leftover ham

• 1½ pounds cooked, ground ham	680 g
• 1 pound ground turkey	455 g
• 2 eggs	
• 1 cup seasoned breadcrumbs	120 g
• 2 teaspoons chicken seasoning	10 ml

Combine ground ham, ground turkey, eggs, seasoned breadcrumb and chicken seasoning in bowl and mix well.

Use hands to pick up loaf mixture and shape into short loaf that will fit into sprayed, oval slow cooker.

Cover and cook on LOW for 4 to 5 hours. Serve with Cherry Sauce.

Cherry Sauce:

• 1 cup cherry preserves	320 g
• 2 tablespoons cider vinegar	30 ml
• Scant ⅛ teaspoon ground cloves	.5 ml
• Scant ⅛ teaspoon ground cinnamon	.5 ml

Place cherry preserves, vinegar, cloves and cinnamon in saucepan and heat. Serve over slices of Ham Loaf. Serves 4 to 6.

Special Ham Supper

- 2½ cups cooked, ground ham   350 g
- ⅔ cup finely crushed cheese crackers   40 g
- 1 large egg
- ⅓ cup hot and spicy ketchup   90 g
- ¼ cup (½ stick) butter   60 g
- 1 (18 ounce) package frozen hash-brown potatoes, thawed   510 g
- 1 onion, coarsely chopped
- 1 (5 ounce) can evaporated milk   150 ml
- 1½ cups shredded Monterey Jack cheese   175 g
- ½ teaspoon paprika   2 ml

Combine ground ham, crackers, egg and ketchup in bowl and shape into 6 patties.

Melt butter in skillet and cook potatoes and onion on medium heat for about 10 minutes. Turn frequently to prevent browning. Drain and transfer to sprayed slow cooker.

Combine milk, cheese, paprika and a little salt and pepper in bowl. Pour mixture over potatoes and onions.

Place ham patties on top; cover and cook on LOW for 3 to 5 hours. Serves 6.

Dressed-Up Hash Browns

- 1 (26 ounce) package frozen hash-brown potatoes with onions and peppers ... 740 g
- Canola oil
- 2 - 3 cups cooked, chopped ham ... 280 - 420 g
- 1 (16 ounce) carton sour cream ... 455 g
- 1 (8 ounce) package shredded cheddar Jack cheese ... 225 g
- 1 (3 ounce) can french-fried onions ... 85 g

Cook potatoes in a little oil in large skillet. Transfer to sprayed 5 to 6-quart (5 to 6 L) slow cooker.

Combine ham, sour cream and cheese in bowl and mix into hash browns. Cover and cook on LOW for 2 to 3 hours.

Dress up potatoes by sprinkling fried onions on top of cheese. Serves 4 to 6.

Ham and Potato Dish

- 4 large baking potatoes, peeled
- 3 cups cubed leftover ham ... 420 g
- 1 (10 ounce) box frozen whole kernel corn, drained ... 280 g
- 1 (10 ounce) package frozen onion-pepper blend, thawed ... 280 g
- 1 teaspoon seasoned salt ... 5 ml
- 2 (10 ounce) cans fiesta nacho cheese soup ... 2 (280 g)
- ½ cup milk ... 125 ml
- 1 (3 ounce) can fried onion rings ... 85 g

Cut potatoes into 1-inch (2.5 cm) cubes. Combine potatoes, ham, corn, onions and peppers and seasoned salt in sprayed slow cooker.

Heat cheese soup and milk in saucepan just enough to mix well. Add to slow cooker and mix with ingredients.

Cover and cook on LOW for 5 to 6 hours or until potatoes are tender.

When ready to serve, sprinkle onions over top. Serves 4 to 6.

Ben's Ham and Rice

- 1 (6.7 ounce) box brown rice-wild rice-mushrooms   170 g
- 3 - 4 cups cooked, chopped or cubed ham   420 - 560 g
- 1 (4 ounce) can sliced mushrooms, drained   115 g
- 1 (10 ounce) package frozen green peas   280 g
- 2 cups chopped celery   200 g

Combine rice, seasoning packet, ham, mushrooms, peas, celery plus 2⅔ cups (650 ml) water in sprayed 4 to 5-quart (4 to 5 L) slow cooker. Stir to mix well.

Cover and cook on LOW for 2 to 4 hours. Serves 4 to 6.

Old-Fashioned Hoppin' John

- 3 (15 ounce) cans black-eyed peas with liquid   3 (425 g)
- 1 onion, chopped
- 1 (6 ounce) package parmesan-butter rice   170 g
- 2 cups cooked, chopped ham   280 g
- 2 tablespoons butter, melted   30 g

Combine peas, onion, rice mix, ham, butter and 1¾ cups (425 ml) water in sprayed slow cooker and mix well.

Cover and cook on LOW for 2 to 4 hours. Serves 6 to 8.

Creamy Potatoes and Ham

- 5 medium potatoes, peeled, sliced, divided
- 1 onion, chopped, divided
- 2 cups cooked, cubed ham, divided   280 g
- 1 (8 ounce) package cubed Velveeta® cheese, divided   225 g
- 1 (10 ounce) can broccoli-cheese soup   280 g
- ¼ cup milk   60 ml

Layer half potatoes, 1 teaspoon (5 ml) salt, half onion, half ham and half cheese in sprayed slow cooker and repeat layers.

Combine soup and milk in bowl until fairly smooth and spoon over layers.

Cover and cook on HIGH for 1 hour. Reduce heat to LOW and cook for 6 to 7 hours. Serves 4.

Creamed Ham with Spaghetti

- 2 (10 ounce) cans cream of mushroom soup with roasted garlic   2 (280 g)
- 1 cup sliced fresh mushrooms   70 g
- 2 - 2½ cups cooked, cubed ham   280 - 350 g
- 1 (5 ounce) can evaporated milk   150 ml
- 1 (7 ounce) box ready-cut spaghetti   200 g

Combine soups, mushrooms, ham, evaporated milk and a little salt and pepper in sprayed slow cooker.

Cover and cook on LOW for 2 hours and mix well.

Cook spaghetti in saucepan and drain. Add spaghetti to slow cooker and toss to coat. Serves 4 to 6.

Rival Manufacturing Company was the first to manufacture slow cookers and introduced slow cookers in 1971. They called the invention a Crock-Pot®, a registered trademark.

Soda Pop Ham

• 4 - 5 pound butt or shank ham	1.8 - 2.3 kg
• ½ cup packed brown sugar	110 g
• 2 teaspoons dijon-style mustard	10 ml
• 1 teaspoon prepared horseradish sauce	5 ml
• ½ cup cola soda	125 ml

Place ham in sprayed slow cooker. Mix brown sugar, mustard and horseradish sauce and rub onto ham. Pour into slow cooker.

Cover and cook on LOW for about 8 to 10 hours or until ham is very tender. Serves about 10.

Ham to the Rescue

• 2½ cups cooked, ground ham	350 g
• ⅔ cup crushed white cheddar Cheez-Its® crackers	40 g
• 1 large egg	
• ⅓ cup chili sauce	90 g
• 4 medium potatoes, peeled, sliced	
• Canola oil	
• 1 green bell pepper, cored, seeded, julienned	
• 1 (8 ounce) package shredded cheddar-Jack cheese	225 g
• 1 (5 ounce) can evaporated milk	150 ml
• 1 teaspoon seasoned salt	5 ml

Combine ham, crushed crackers, egg and chili sauce in bowl and mix well. Shape ham mixture into 6 patties and set aside.

Saute potatoes in a little oil in skillet and turn several times to brown lightly on both sides. Place potatoes and bell pepper in sprayed 6-quart (6 L) slow cooker.

In separate bowl, combine cheese, evaporated milk and seasoned salt and pour over potatoes. Place ham patties over potatoes.

Cover and cook on LOW for 3 to 4 hours. Serves 4 to 6.

Ham and Potato Casserole

- 3 - 4 large potatoes, peeled, thinly sliced
- 1 (8 ounce) package shredded cheddar cheese — 225 g
- ½ cup chopped onion — 80 g
- ½ cup chopped green bell pepper — 75 g
- 2 ribs celery, sliced
- 2 cups cooked, chopped ham — 280 g
- 1 (10 ounce) can cream of chicken soup — 280 g
- ⅔ cup milk — 150 ml
- 1 teaspoon seasoned salt — 5 ml

Place potatoes, cheese onion, bell pepper, celery and ham in sprayed slow cooker and mix well.

Combine soup, milk and seasoned salt in small bowl and pour evenly over potato-vegetable mixture.

Cover and cook on HIGH for 4 hours. Serves 8.

Sweet-and-Sour Sausage Links

- 2 (16 ounce) packages miniature smoked sausage links — 2 (455 g)
- ¾ cup chili sauce — 205 g
- 1 cup packed brown sugar — 220 g
- ¼ cup horseradish — 55 g

Place sausages in sprayed 4-quart (4 L) slow cooker. Combine chili sauce, brown sugar and horseradish in bowl and pour over sausages.

Cover and cook on LOW for 4 hours. Serves 4 to 6.

TIP: This can be served as an appetizer or served over hot, cooked rice.

If cooking soups or stews, leave at least a 2-inch (5 cm) space between the top of the cooker and the food so that the recipe can come to a simmer and not boil over.

Tortellini Italian-Style

- **2 pounds bulk Italian sausage** — 910 g
- **1 (15 ounce) carton refrigerated marinara sauce** — 425 g
- **2 cups sliced fresh mushrooms, sliced** — 145 g
- **1 (15 ounce) cans Italian stewed tomatoes** — 425 g
- **1 (9 ounce) package refrigerated cheese tortellini** — 255 g
- **1½ cups shredded mozzarella cheese** — 170 g

Brown and cook sausage in skillet for 10 to 15 minutes and drain well.

Combine sausage, marinara sauce, mushrooms and tomatoes in sprayed 5-quart (5 L) slow cooker.

Cover and cook on LOW 6 to 7 hours. Stir in tortellini.

Cover and cook on HIGH for about 15 minutes or until tortellini is tender. When ready to serve, sprinkle with cheese. Serves 4 to 6.

Cooking time on HIGH equals about half the cooking time on LOW.

Stewed Tomato, Sausage and Rice

- **1 (16 ounce) Polish sausage ring, cut into ¼ inch slices**   455/6 mm
- **2 (15 ounce) cans Italian stewed tomatoes**   2 (425 g)
- **1 (16 ounce) package frozen chopped onions and bell peppers**   455 g
- **2 ribs celery, sliced**
- **1 teaspoon Italian seasoning**   5 ml
- **1 teaspoon dried basil**   5 ml
- **½ teaspoon hot pepper sauce**   2 ml
- **1½ cups instant rice**   145 g

Layer sausage, stewed tomatoes, onions and bell peppers, and celery in sprayed slow cooker.

Sprinkle with Italian seasoning, basil and pepper sauce. Cover and cook on LOW for 7 hours.

Stir in rice and ½ cup (125 ml) water and cook for additional 30 minutes. Serves 4 to 5.

Sausage and Beans

- 1 (1 pound) fully cooked smoked, link sausage — 455 g
- 2 (15 ounce) cans baked beans — 2 (425 g)
- 1 (15 ounce) can great northern beans, drained — 425 g
- 1 (15 ounce) can pinto beans, drained — 425 g
- ½ cup chili sauce — 135 g
- ⅔ cup packed brown sugar — 150 g
- 1 tablespoon Worcestershire sauce — 15 ml

Cut link sausage into 1-inch (2.5 cm) slices. Layer sausage and beans in sprayed slow cooker.

Combine chili sauce, brown sugar, a little black pepper and Worcestershire sauce in bowl and pour over beans and sausage.

Cover and cook on LOW for 4 hours. Stir before serving. Serves 4.

Sauerkraut and Bratwurst

- 1 (28 ounce) jar refrigerated sauerkraut — 795 g
- ¾ cup beer — 175 ml
- 1 tablespoon marinade for chicken — 15 ml
- 1 (1 ounce) packet onion soup mix — 30 g
- 2 pounds pre-cooked bratwurst — 910 g

Combine sauerkraut, beer, marinade for chicken and onion soup mix in sprayed 4 to 5-quart (4 to 5 L) slow cooker and mix well.

Cut bratwurst in diagonal slices and place on top of sauerkraut-beer mixture.

Cover and cook on LOW for 5 to 6 hours or on HIGH for 2 hours 30 minutes to 3 hours. Serves 4 to 6.

Sauerkraut-Kielbasa Supper

- 1 (48 ounce) can sauerkraut with liquid   1.4 kg
- 2 pounds precooked kielbasa sausage, sliced   910 g
- 2 onions, sliced
- 2 ribs celery, chopped

Layer half of sauerkraut, sausage, onion and celery in slow cooker and repeat layers with remaining ingredients. Cook on LOW for 6 to 8 hours. Serves 4 to 6.

Kielbasa with Potatoes and Cabbage

- 3 - 4 medium new (red) potatoes with peels, sliced
- 2 onions, sliced
- 3 carrots, sliced
- 2 cups chopped green cabbage   140 g
- ¼ cup Italian dressing   60 ml
- 1 (1 pound) kielbasa sausage   455 g
- 1 (15 ounce) can Italian stewed tomatoes   425 g

Place potatoes, onions, carrots, cabbage and Italian dressing in sprayed, large slow cooker.

Cut sausage into 1-inch (2.5 cm) pieces and place on top of vegetables. Drizzle stewed tomatoes in even layers over vegetables.

Cover and cook on LOW for 6 to 8 hours or until vegetables are tender. Serves 4 to 6.

Bacon-Spinach Breakfast Dish

- 4 cups chopped bread pieces with crusts ... 140 g
- 1 pound bacon ... 455 g
- 1 (10 ounce) box frozen spinach, thawed ... 280 g
- 1 (12 ounce) carton button mushrooms, sliced ... 340 g
- 8 eggs
- ½ cup milk ... 125 ml
- 1 cup shredded cheddar cheese ... 115 g

Drop bread pieces into slow cooker. Fry bacon in skillet, drain on paper towels and save 1 to 2 tablespoons (15 to 30 ml) bacon drippings. Crumble bacon over bread.

Squeeze spinach between paper towels to drain completely. Saute mushrooms and spinach in bacon drippings and pour over bacon. Beat eggs and milk in separate bowl.

Pour over mushroom-spinach mixture. Sprinkle cheese on top and cook on LOW for 2 to 3 hours or until eggs are firm. Serves 8 to 10.

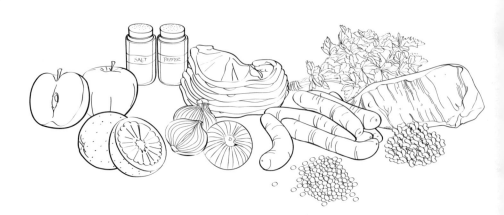

Desserts

Pineapple-Rice Pudding

- 1 cup cooked white rice   185 g
- ¾ cup sugar   150 g
- 1 (1 pint) carton half-and-half cream   500 ml
- 1 tablespoon cornstarch   15 ml
- 3 eggs, beaten
- 1 teaspoon vanilla   5 ml
- 1 (15 ounce) can crushed pineapple with juice   425 g
- Pecan, chopped, toasted

Combine rice, sugar and half-and-half cream in bowl and mix well. Stir cornstarch into eggs while beating and add vanilla and pineapple.

Pour into sprayed 4 to 5-quart (4 to 5 L) slow cooker. Cover and cook on LOW for 2 to 3 hours.

When ready to serve, top each serving with toasted, chopped pecans as a special touch. Serves 6.

Mocha Rice Pudding

• 4 cups cooked white rice	630 g
• 2 (12 ounce) cans evaporated milk	2 (355 ml)
• ½ - ¾ cup sugar	100 - 150 g
• ¼ cup cocoa	20 g
• ¼ cup (½ stick) butter, melted	55 g
• 1 teaspoon vanilla	5 ml

Pour all ingredients in sprayed slow cooker and stir well. Cover and cook on LOW for 3 to 4 hours or until flavors blend and rice is pudding consistency. Serve warm or cold. Serves 4 to 6.

Delicious Bread Pudding

• 8 cups cubed leftover hot rolls, cinnamon rolls or bread	280 g
• 2 cups milk	500 ml
• 4 large eggs	
• ¾ cup sugar	150 g
• ⅓ cup packed brown sugar	75 g
• ¼ cup (½ stick) butter, melted	60 g
• 1 teaspoon vanilla	5 ml
• ¼ teaspoon ground nutmeg	1 ml
• 1 cup finely chopped pecans	110 g
• Lemon sauce or frozen whipped topping, thawed	

Place cubed bread or rolls in sprayed slow cooker. Combine, milk, eggs, sugar, brown sugar, butter, vanilla and nutmeg in bowl and beat until smooth.

Stir in pecans. Add to slow cooker. Cover and cook on LOW for 3 hours. Serve with lemon sauce or whipped topping. Serves 6.

Bread Pudding with Coconut and Nuts

- **1 cup sugar** — 200 g
- **½ cup (1 stick) butter, softened** — 115 g
- **1 teaspoon ground cinnamon** — 5 ml
- **4 eggs**
- **3 cups white bread cubes** — 105 g
- **⅓ cup flaked coconut** — 30 g
- **⅓ cup chopped pecans** — 40 g

Beat sugar, butter and cinnamon in bowl. Add eggs and beat well until it blends. Stir in bread, coconut and pecans. Pour into sprayed 4 to 5-quart (4 to 5 L) slow cooker.

Cover and cook on LOW for 3 to 4 hours or on HIGH 1 hour 30 minutes to 2 hours or until knife inserted in center comes out clean. Serves 8.

TIP: Serve pudding warm with caramel ice cream topping, if desired.

Baked Apples

- **4 - 5 large baking apples**
- **1 tablespoon lemon juice**   **15 ml**
- **⅓ cup Craisins®**   **40 g**
- **½ cup chopped pecans**   **55 g**
- **¾ cup packed brown sugar**   **165 g**
- **½ teaspoon ground cinnamon**   **2 ml**
- **¼ cup (½ stick) butter, melted**   **60 g**
- **Caramel ice cream topping**

Scoop out center of each apple and leave cavity about ½-inch (1.2 cm) from bottom.

Peel top of apples down about 1-inch (2.5 cm) and brush lemon juice on peeled edges.

Combine Craisins®, pecans, brown sugar, cinnamon and butter in bowl. Spoon mixture into apple cavities.

Pour ½ cup (125 ml) water in sprayed, oval slow cooker and place apples on bottom. Cover and cook on LOW for 1 to 3 hours or until tender.

Serve warm or room temperature drizzled with caramel ice cream topping. Serves 5.

Red Hot Caramel Apples

- 6 gala apples
- ¾ cup packed light brown sugar   55 g
- 1 (1 ounce) box Red Hots® cinnamon candies   30 g
- 18 caramel candies
- Cinnamon
- Sugar
- Frozen whipped topping, thawed

Cut off stem end of apples, carefully cut around core and remove, but do not cut all the way through bottom. Place 1 caramel candy in bottom of apple.

Divide equally among apples the brown sugar, red hots and remaining caramels. Top caramel may stick out, but it will melt over outside of apple.

Sprinkle cinnamon and sugar liberally on top. Place apples in sprayed slow cooker. Cover and cook on LOW for 4 to 5 hours or until caramel melts and apples are tender. Serve with whipped topping. Serves 6 to 8.

Butter-Baked Apples

- 6 large green baking apples
- 2 tablespoons lemon juice   30 ml
- ¼ cup (½ stick) butter, melted   60 g
- 1 cup packed brown sugar   220 g
- 1 teaspoon ground cinnamon   5 ml
- ½ teaspoon ground nutmeg   2 ml
- Vanilla ice cream

Peel, core, cut apples in half and place in sprayed slow cooker. Drizzle with lemon juice and butter. Sprinkle with brown sugar, cinnamon and nutmeg.

Cover and cook on LOW for 2 hours 30 minutes to 3 hours 30 minutes or on HIGH for 1 hour 30 minutes to 2 hours. Serve with vanilla ice cream. Serves 6.

Cran-Apples for Pound Cake

- 1 (6 ounce) package dried apples   170 g
- ½ cup Craisins®
- 3 cups cranberry juice cocktail   710 ml
- ¾ cup packed brown sugar   180 ml
- 2 cinnamon sticks, halved
- Pound cake or vanilla ice cream

Add apples, Craisins®, juice, brown sugar and cinnamon sticks to sprayed 3 to 4-quart (3 to 4 L) slow cooker.

Cover and cook on LOW for 4 to 5 hours or until liquid absorbs and fruit is tender.

Serve warm, at room temperature or chilled over slices of pound cake or vanilla ice cream. Serves 6.

Praline-Apple Crisp

- 6 cups peeled, cored, sliced gala or granny smith apples
- 2 teaspoons cinnamon
- 1 teaspoon sugar
- ½ cup (1 stick) butter
- ⅓ cup packed brown sugar
- ½ cup quick-cooking oats
- ¼ cup flour
- ½ cup chopped pecans
- ½ cup toffee bits

Place apples with cinnamon and sugar and place in sprayed slow cooker. In separate bowl, mix butter, brown sugar, oats and flour. Batter will be lumpy and crumbly.

Stir in chopped pecans and toffee bits. Spoon mixture over apples as evenly as possible. Cover and cook on LOW for 5 to 6 hours. Serve when apple are tender. Serves 4 to 6.

Peachy-Cranberry Delight

- 1½ cups quick-cooking oats — 120 g
- 1 (1 pound) box brown sugar — 455 g
- ⅔ cup sugar — 135 g
- ¾ cup biscuit mix — 90 g
- 2 teaspoons ground cinnamon — 10 ml
- ½ cup orange juice — 125 ml
- 1 (16 ounce) package frozen sliced peaches, thawed — 455 g
- 1 (6 ounce) package Craisins® — 170 g

Combine oats, brown sugar, sugar, biscuit mix, cinnamon and orange juice in large bowl. Gently stir in peaches and Craisins®. Spoon into sprayed slow cooker.

Cover and cook on LOW for 5 hours. Serve while still warm. Serves 10.

Fresh Peach Cobbler

- 1 cup sugar — 200 g
- ¾ cup biscuit mix — 90 g
- 2 eggs
- 2 teaspoons vanilla — 10 ml
- 1 (5 ounce) can evaporated milk — 145 g
- 2 tablespoons butter, melted — 30 g
- 3 large, ripe peaches, peeled, mashed
- Peach ice cream

Combine sugar and biscuit mix in large bowl, stir in eggs, vanilla, evaporated milk and butter and mix well.

Fold in peaches, pour into sprayed slow cooker and stir well. Cover and cook on LOW for 6 to 8 hours or on HIGH for 3 to 4 hours.

Serve warm with peach ice cream. Serves 6.

Peaches with Crunch

- ¾ cup old-fashioned oats   60 g
- ⅔ cup packed brown sugar   150 g
- ¾ cup sugar   150 g
- ½ cup biscuit mix   60 g
- ½ teaspoon ground cinnamon   2 ml
- 2 (15 ounce) cans sliced peaches, well drained   2 (425 g)

Combine oats, brown sugar, sugar, biscuit mix and cinnamon in bowl. Stir in drained peaches and spoon into sprayed 3 to 4-quart (3 to 4 L) slow cooker.

Cover and cook on LOW for 4 to 5 hours. Serve in sherbet dishes. Serves 6.

Surprise Dessert

- 1 (18 ounce) box spice cake mix   510 g
- 1 cup butterscotch chips   170 g
- 4 eggs, slightly beaten
- ¾ cup canola oil   175 ml
- 1 (3.4 ounce) package butterscotch instant pudding mix   100 g
- 1 (8 ounce) carton sour cream   225 g
- 1 cup chopped pecans   110 g
- Butter-pecan ice cream

Combine all ingredients and ¾ cup (175 ml) water in large bowl. Pour into sprayed 4 to 5-quart (4 to 5 L) slow cooker.

Cover and cook on LOW for 6 to 7 hours or on HIGH for 3 hours to 3 hours 30 minutes. Serve hot or room temperature with butter-pecan ice cream. Serves 8.

Slow cookers work best when filled to between two-thirds and three-quarters of capacity. Filling a cooker to the brim will prevent even cooking and will require a longer cooking time.

Chocolate Delight

- 1 (18 ounce) box chocolate cake mix   510 g
- 1 (8 ounce) carton sour cream 225 g
- 4 eggs
- ¾ cup canola oil   175 ml
- 1 (3.4 ounce) box instant chocolate pudding mix   100 g
- ¾ cup chopped pecans   85 g
- Vanilla ice cream

Mix cake mix, sour cream, eggs, oil, pudding mix, pecans and 1 cup (250 ml) water in bowl. Pour into sprayed slow cooker.

Cover and cook on LOW for 6 to 8 hours. Serve hot or warm with vanilla ice cream. Serves 8.

Chocolate Fondue

Use the slow cooker as a fondue pot.

- 2 (7 ounce) chocolate bars, chopped   2 (200 g)
- 2 (2 ounce) bars white chocolate, chopped   2 (55 g)
- 1 (7 ounce) jar marshmallow creme   200 g
- ¾ cup half-and-half cream   175 ml
- ½ cup slivered almonds, chopped, toasted   40 g
- ¼ cup amaretto liqueur   60 ml
- Pound cake

Combine broken chocolate bars, white chocolate bar, marshmallow creme, half-and-half cream and almonds in sprayed, small slow cooker.

Cover and cook on LOW for about 2 hours or until chocolates melt. Stir to mix well and fold in amaretto. Serve 6 to 8.

TIP: Use slow cooker as fondue pot or transfer chocolate mixture to fondue pot. Cut pound cake into small squares and use to dip into fondue.

Fruit Sauce

- **8 cups fresh fruit, thinly sliced**   1.9 L
- **1 cup orange juice**   250 ml
- **⅓ cup packed brown sugar**   75 g
- **⅓ cup sugar**   70 g
- **2 tablespoons quick-cooking tapioca**   30 ml
- **1 teaspoon grated fresh ginger**   5 ml
- **⅔ cup Craisins® or cherries**   80 g
- **Pound cake or ice cream**

Combine fruit, juice, brown sugar, sugar, tapioca and ginger in sprayed 4-quart (4 L) slow cooker. Cover and cook on LOW for 4 hours. Add Craisins® or cherries and mix well.

Cover and let stand for 10 to 15 minutes. To serve, spoon over slices of pound cake or ice cream. Serves 8.

Recipes in this cookbook may be cooked in 3 to 6-quart slow cookers. You may need to adjust the quantity of ingredients for a smaller cooker.

Fruit Compote Sauce

- **3 gala or Granny Smith apples, peeled, cored, sliced**
- **1 teaspoon cinnamon**   **5 ml**
- **½ cup dried sweetened cranberries or Craisins®**   **60g**
- **½ cup dried apricot halves**   **75 g**
- **1 (8 ounce) can pineapple tidbits with unsweetened juice**   **225 g**
- **¾ cup orange juice**   **175 ml**
- **¼ cup sugar**   **50 g**
- **1 (20 ounce) can peach pie filling**   **565 g**
- **Ice cream, pound cake or angel food cake**

Place apples in sprayed slow cooker and sprinkle cinnamon over top. Mix cranberries, apricots and pineapple chunks and pour over apples. Pour orange juice over mixture.

Cover and cook on LOW for 4 to 5 hours.

Add peach pie filling to slow cooker, stir and cook about 30 minutes to heat throughout. Serve over ice cream, pound cake or angel food cake. Serves 4 to 6.

Magnificent Fudge

- **2 (16 ounce) jars slightly salted, dry-roasted peanuts**   **2 (455 g)**
- **1 (12 ounce) package semi-sweet chocolate chips**   **340 g**
- **1 (4 ounce) bar German chocolate, broken**   **115 g**
- **2 (24 ounce) packages white chocolate bark or (3 pounds) almond bark, chopped**   **680 g/1.3 kg**

Place peanuts in sprayed 5-quart (5 L) slow cooker. In layers, add chocolate chips, German chocolate and white chocolate bark.

Cover and cook on LOW for 3 hours without removing lid. When candy cooks 3 hours, remove lid, stir and cool in covered slow cooker.

Stir again and drop teaspoonfuls onto wax paper. Serves 8 to 12.

TIP: For darker fudge, use 1 white bark and 1 dark bark. DO NOT STIR.

Index

Index

C

Chicken & Turkey Main Dishes

281

Index

Index

Index

Index

Index

Index

Index